THE POWER OF
SCRIPTWRITING!

THE POWER OF SCRIPTWRITING!

TEACHING ESSENTIAL WRITING SKILLS THROUGH PODCASTS, GRAPHIC NOVELS, MOVIES, AND MORE

PETER GUTIÉRREZ

TEACHERS COLLEGE PRESS

TEACHERS COLLEGE | COLUMBIA UNIVERSITY

NEW YORK AND LONDON

Published by Teachers College Press, 1234 Amsterdam Avenue, New York, NY 10027

Library of Congress Cataloging-in-Publication Data

Gutierrez, Peter.
  The power of scriptwriting!– teaching essential writing skills through podcasts, graphic novels, movies, and more: / Peter Gutiérrez.
      pages cm
  Includes bibliographical references and index.

    1. Language arts–Curricula–United States. 2. Language arts–Standards–United States. 3. English language–Composition and exercises–Study and teaching–United States. 4. Film adaptations–Authorship. 5. Motion picture authorship–Study and teaching. 6. Graphic novels in education. I. Title.
  LB1576.G88 2013
  808'.042071–dc23   2013020391

ISBN 978-0-8077-5466-5 (paper)
eISBN 978-0-8077-7275-1

Printed on acid-free paper
Manufactured in the United States of America

CONTENTS

Introduction:
Invisible Texts Made Visible

Are you concerned about motivating students to write in a world that seems to value books and traditional forms of text less and less in favor of a range of ever-changing **media**? After all, students today are perhaps more likely to curl up with a mobile device that streams their favorite movie or TV show than with, say, a paperback. And even when they are reading in the conventional sense, those texts are not always chapter books and YA titles like those we grew up with but often something like the digitized versions of hit manga titles. How, then, to connect independent reading and personal meaningfulness to in-school, curriculum-driven composition, especially creative writing, a link that at one time seemed intuitive?

Well, the good news is that young people today actually *do* live and breathe good ol' print-based text, even when they're not aware of the fact. That's because most of the main types of popular entertainment start with the written word in the form of **scripts**. It's natural, though, that some students may not realize this. After all, with rare exceptions, scripts are not widely published, and their writers often take a backseat to famous characters, **directors**, or "TV personalities." This is why the highly readable texts that these writers create—texts that have the power to inspire if treated like exemplars—remain largely invisible.

As proof, just try asking students where all the content they enjoy comes from; chances are, they have never read a script from their favorite TV or comic book series. Some younger students may even be under the impression that in such cases "words" are afterthoughts in the creative process. Or, if students realize that scripts do play a vital role in the media they love, they may feel that they're highly technical documents, full of jargon and weird formatting, more like user manuals or annual reports than something they themselves would ever want to write.

That's where this book comes in. You can use its ideas and resources to add media-based writing—scriptwriting—easily and impactfully to your curriculum.

WHO SHOULD READ THIS BOOK

The time is certainly ripe for scriptwriting. It is already common to help students create **digital stories** and **videos** to enhance a range of literacies (Miller,

2010), to embrace the idea of writing across the curriculum (Condon & Rutz, 2012), and to introduce writing **comics** as a practice that can bolster student understanding of everything from narrative structure to punctuation (NCTE, 2005). And these are just three of the topics covered in the chapters that follow. So if you're thinking of doing these sorts of things or already using scripts in the classroom in the form of more traditional practices such as reading and performing Shakespeare or Reader's Theatre, then this book is for you. That's because the goal here is to unify what are typically presented as disparate writing products into a single compositional discipline, thus allowing it to be taught in a coherent way while demonstrating its relevance and real-world authenticity to students.

Moreover, the versatility of scriptwriting—the media, topics, and writing products that it can address—means that it not only can reinforce important curricular objectives but engage and support students who otherwise may struggle with writing for one reason or another. For example, the combination of visuals and oral language that is central to many types of scripts provides a natural form of scaffolding and therefore can be helpful in terms of teaching English Language Learners (Echevarria, Vogt, & Short, 2004).

Scripts Support the *Entire* Writing Curriculum

The assertion in the section head above might not seem so bold when one considers that scriptwriting is not *just* a subset of creative writing or narrative writing; it encompasses all modes. In fact, it's not even a genre of writing—that would be like saying "bookwriting" is a genre. Books can cover any topic and do so on a modest or vast scale, featuring a variety of tones and purposes. The same can be said for scripts.

More important, scriptwriting can build motivation for writing more generally by changing a young person's notion of what constitutes writing. Indeed, scriptwriting can be a game-changer for students who, though proficient in composition, don't approach writing in a way that delivers on their full potential or allows them to consider themselves "writers."

It's tempting to think, then, that we're back at the issue of engagement again. However, the aim here is not merely to introduce students to a brand-new type of writing that they'll simply like more than the "old" types of writing they've been doing. Rather, sound writing strategies, pedagogy, and practices are valid *across* **formats**. So, yes, writing scripts can be very different from writing prose, but the important thing to keep in mind is that the principles for success in both forms of text are the same.

First, there are parameters, both in content and form, in writing scripts, and there are certain trade-offs involved when one decides to move into this area— much as there are when many new forms of text are introduced into classrooms: Most of the important "rules" of writing prose still apply, some don't, and there are several new things to learn as well. So while writing an expository script for a **news spot** (see Chapters 2 and 5), a writer must still research and organize a large set of facts but now has the additional challenge of making the content aurally or visually engaging whenever possible. At the same time, this writer *gets* to use **sound effects** (SFX) or **graphics** to convey information on a scale and with a complexity that might be inappropriate, if not impossible, when composing a conventional prose text. Interestingly, many of scriptwriting's constraints and rewards happen to be shared by another form of literature that is routinely read, studied, and written in schools: stage plays.

Sure, scriptwriting has its own conventions that do not appear in more common forms of text, but this does not make it inherently complex or difficult to implement. For instance consider how, like scripts, poetry has conventions that do not appear in prose; yet is it widely known that composing poetry greatly enhances students' appreciation of language and storytelling and, most important, helps develop their personal, self-expressive "meaning-making" in the form of writing (Hanauer & Rivers, 2004).

The bottom line is, having taught various forms of scriptwriting since the early 1990s, I can confidently say that there is nothing like seeing students for whom extended writing was previously a chore suddenly experience an awakening when it comes to scripts. Their focus becomes laser like even as their eyes widen in response to a new realm of creative possibilities opening up to them. Writing no longer becomes a matter of staring at a blank sheet of paper or a computer screen. Sketches are quickly made on odd scraps of paper, muffled giggling can be heard here and there, and hands shoot up with urgent questions. Most gratifying of all, there's an overwhelming urge to share one's writing—even one's plans for writing—with others. In short, the joy of writing, and reading, comes vibrantly to life.

In this light, then, the fact that scriptwriting can aid the teaching and learning of a vast range of curricular skills is just a bonus.

Engagement, Media Literacy, and Learning Styles

When students learn about how scripts are written and then practice scriptwriting themselves, they get a behind-the-scenes glimpse of media techniques and production. This knowledge can transform their understanding of other texts they encounter both in school and outside of school—making students more media literate. For example, by grasping how scriptwriters compose for different audiences and purposes, students will learn about the parameters and formal elements of diverse media and discover more about the jobs of those who collaborate with scriptwriters—actors, directors, **Foley artists**, editors, and **producers**. (Are any of your students interested in pursuing these as vocations or avocations? If so, scriptwriting provides a powerful vehicle for connecting these skills and talents to the writing curriculum.)

At the same time, media-based writing represents an authentic and powerful way to tackle problem-solving and decision-making skills. All scriptwriters—students and professionals alike—constantly grapple with questions like, how can I convey story elements indirectly, using devices such as sound? How can I use the script format and specialized vocabulary to help readers of the script see the same mental images that I do? Is my writing sufficiently clear for those who may help produce my video or graphic novel—and are the choices I've made realistic in terms of ability, budget, and other real-world factors?

As an added benefit, repeated practice at making such decisions helps develop students' ability to *read* media messages; once students better understand the questions of production that creators must invariably make, they become more sensitive to how these questions have been answered in any given media product and thus become more critical consumers of such products. This in turn has numerous benefits: In the context of school, media literacy has been shown to improve literacy overall, and outside of school, it reduces the likelihood of unhealthy eating habits, drug use, and criminal behavior (Kaiser Family Foundation, 2003).

Yet while sharpened media literacy and critical-thinking skills are welcome byproducts of introducing scriptwriting to your classroom, it's important not to lose track of, well, the fun. After all, the obvious reason to inject scriptwriting into the curriculum is to engage students.

Of course the trick is not to stop at fun and engagement alone. The goal, again, is to support the writing curriculum by coming at the same concepts, strategies, skills, and processes already taught but from a new direction. This provides a means of reinforcement for all students and, perhaps more important, a way to reach some students who had trouble either conceptualizing or implementing these skills in the first place. Specifically, the writing process involved in creating scripts—in its brainstorming, drafting, revision, rehearsal, second revision, and performance stages—offers new opportunities to reach students with the following multiple intelligences, per Howard Gardner's work (2011), and tie their talents to language-based texts in powerful ways. No, research on learning styles has not "shown conclusively that students learn better when they are taught according to their preferred modality" (Stansbury, 2010, p. 1), but in the context of motivation alone, the option to teach and learn along various pathways and modalities can only help in terms of *inspiring* students to write; in short, it's not about teaching "content" but sparking excitement to learn compositional techniques and strategies like those below, which are related to several of the multiple intelligences identified by Gardner:

- *Logical-mathematical* ("number/reasoning smart"): Scripts are highly structured, and writers must constantly figure out how to tell stories within established quantifiable parameters (e.g., a particular page count for a comic or available running time or air time for an **audio** or video **podcast**).

- *Spatial* ("picture smart"): Visualization, in both internal and external modes (i.e., what writers see in their minds *and* what audiences ultimately see), is key to scriptwriting.
- *Bodily-kinesthetic* ("body smart") and *Musical* ("music smart"): Scriptwriters must consider spoken language and sound more broadly; and they often act out draft text for staging purposes.
- *Interpersonal* ("people smart"): Almost by definition, scriptwriters can't work in total isolation–for the public to experience their work, others must be involved in shaping it, and writers compose with these collaborators in mind.

With all students, however, the goal is to leverage their engagement with certain kinds of media texts to explore, analyze, compose, and produce them with the same rigor and disciplinary tools that we'd expect anywhere in the curriculum.

TESOL Opportunities: Scriptwriting and English Language Learners

Writing scripts also provides a multitude of ways to engage and support the ELLs in your classroom. After all, many of them will already be familiar with the media products covered in this book through examples in their native language (in addition, of course, to English-language media examples), and you can build from this common source of motivation and prior knowledge. Moreover, if you're a teacher of English to speakers of other languages (TESOL), you can leverage the following benefits of scriptwriting regardless of the **medium** for which students are writing.

- *Speaking and Listening.* You can incorporate opportunities for students to hear and be heard at nearly every step of the scriptwriting process. These include listening closely as peers read their drafts aloud or focusing on oral expression as one reads a part in someone else's script. This abundance of options for oral expression is true even of script formats that are not typically performed. For example, a comic book script can be acted out as a form of Reader's Theatre. The benefits in terms of fluency and comprehension for ELLs make Reader's Theatre an effective teaching strategy, and empowering these students to create the texts that are then performed is an added plus for those students whose proficiency makes it possible (Boothe & Caspary, 2011).
- *Collaboration.* One of the challenges and joys of teaching ELLs is seeing them become more integrated socially and culturally with other students as their communication skills in English improve. The collaborative possibilities of scriptwriting facilitate this process. You can pair native English speakers and nonnative speakers in teams that make use of their different talents or interests, or you can break a more involved

project, such as scripting a multisegment podcast or graphic novel, into meaningful parts that allow individuals to contribute to a group effort. Alternately, ELLs who share a native language can work together to create two versions of the same script—one in that language and a subsequent one in English, much in the way that movies, comics, and TV shows are routinely translated for different audiences.

- *Visual Scaffolding.* Most of the script formats discussed in this book are intensely visual. This will motivate ELLs and increase their self-confidence as they consistently have the option of telling a story or conveying information primarily with images. In this way, students who might otherwise feel that their self-expression is hindered by a weak command of English vocabulary can instead focus on structure, point of view, gathering details, and other important prewriting decisions. Then, with motivation firmly in place, they can work on honing the numerous word-choice skills on which effective scriptwriting is predicated.

In addition to these general suggestions regarding ELLs, be sure to check out the Differentiated Instruction feature in subsequent chapters' Writing Process section for specific strategies.

HOW TO USE THIS BOOK

Organization

How can you make the most of the lessons and projects in the pages that follow? Well, first I should probably clarify that this book is not intended to be a comprehensive reference manual on writing various kinds of scripts from conception through final draft. As with the more general topic of youth media production, entire books could be (and in fact have been) written about each of the types of scripts you'll find in these pages. Nor does this book attempt to lay out a road map for a yearlong writing curriculum in which scripts play a central role (although the Make the Connection boxes provided throughout the book can help you link assignments and skills across different chapters).

Instead, the goal here is to present engaging projects that you can dip into as needed during the course of a school year to support the rest of your writing goals. Still, if you'd like to build scriptwriting into your curriculum as a recurring strand in which student knowledge and comfort levels build with each successive level—the essence of effective literacy scaffolding (Applebee & Langer, 1983)—you'll be able to do that as well. With this in mind, the content is ordered according to a slightly ascending level of complexity, allowing students to leverage what they have already learned, as illustrated in the following chapter descriptions:

Chapter 1: Connecting Stage to Screen. We begin by establishing stage plays as a familiar, foundational writing product that informs the purpose and format of many different script types.

Chapter 2: Spoken Word and Audio Scripts. Although they lack a visual component, audio scripts extend what is a defining question of scripts generally: How does one convey text to an audience by means of an intermediary? After all, radio listeners don't read scripts directly. With this chapter, the practical and technical characteristics of the form become clearer to budding scriptwriters.

Chapter 3: Comics and Graphic Novel Scripts. Comics scripts, such as those for graphic novels, come next as they add an important new element: visual storytelling. Significantly, they do so in a static form that, because it can be so intuitive, enables writers to master certain basic concepts that can serve them well in other media, too.

Chapter 4: Movie and Television Scripts. Writing for film and TV follows logically once students have begun to think about how to create image-based narratives. These scripts combine the need to write for performers (as in audio and stage scripts) with the need to convey information visually (as in comics scripts).

Chapter 5: Digital Storytelling and Video Scripts. Digital stories and short videos can expand upon the lessons of movie and television scriptwriting because students can, and in many cases should, use *existing* media to supplement their crafting of original material. In short, these forms of scriptwriting can rely on *assemblage* that potentially involves the inclusion of static images (such as photos and comics-like artwork), audio **voice-over**, and clips of **moving-image media**—all are fair game.

Chapter 6: Further Adventures in Scriptwriting. Finally, we examine a range of special projects that include everything from live **multimedia** events to picture books and reality TV. Here students have an opportunity to build upon and extend the skills introduced in the previous chapters.

Please note that the goal of each chapter is not necessarily to have students write a long-form work from start to finish—a script for a full-length graphic novel or feature film, for example, requires an extraordinary amount of effort, and your curriculum may not be able to allocate sufficient time for even *one* large-scale project like this. However, students might derive the same instructional benefits—not to mention the self-confidence—to tackle larger projects by writing a given script in an abbreviated form, such as a "mini-comic" or a single **scene** from a TV pilot. Again, the idea is to *support your existing writing curriculum* with the projects you'll find here, not to steer it in a completely different direction.

That's possible because these projects deal with the same modes, strategies, and skills as the rest of your curriculum—however, the projects in this book come at writing and literacy skills in a new way so that students can both conceptualize and practice them differently. One might go as far as to say that this book does not present any new types of writing, only new types of writing *products*. Although technology and media literacy are touched upon throughout, generally, this content should go to the heart of what you teach when you teach writing in its broadest possible sense: how to entertain and/or inform readers in ways that are effective, authentic, and self-expressive.

This book is designed, then, for you to explore as needed. I encourage you to check out not only the chapters that feature scripts that immediately interest you but also the chapters that feature types that you may *not* be interested in simply because the curricular overlap is so great from one medium to another. For example, you may come across an activity in audio scripts that you can apply directly to creating digital storytelling scripts, which might be what you *really* want to teach and which, after all, contains an audio component. In terms of general ELA alignment, you can use the assignments and activities to replace or supplement those in a writing program or basal, or to provide differentiated instruction. When you have a targeted skill to teach, just check the Table of Contents or index to find where it is covered.

To help students become accustomed to the newness of scripts, the annotated writing models in Chapters 2 through 6 can be reproduced and shared. If you want to follow up on these introductory texts, there's certainly no shortage of full-length professional models out there that can be compared point-for-point with the media products that are based on them. This highly instructive process (see Chapter 1) can help students grasp the conventions of any given medium and script format, thus making this book a resource for reading and an easy way to put transliteracy into action.

Curriculum Integration and Common Core State Standards

To help you integrate scriptwriting into your existing writing curriculum, each chapter calls out both the 7th-grade and 11th-/12th-grade Standards for English Language Arts as established by the Common Core State Standards Initiative (National Governors Association Center for Best Practices & Council of Chief State School Officers [NGA Center & CCSSO], 2010). With these anchors in place, I firmly believe that writers as young as those in grade 5 and as seasoned as college students in a composition or 100-level media course can benefit from the skills covered herein.

To be clear, these Common Core State Standards (CCSS) are not without controversy, and I do find myself agreeing with their critics on occasion. That said, the way that they embrace non-print media makes them a perfect fit for scriptwriting, as does their mindfulness of reading and writing in other disciplines. Moreover, as CCSS does seem to be the dominant force in K–12 these days, I'd like to see the top-down flavor often found in their implementation complemented by an emphasis on student creativity and the aforementioned outside-of-school literacies. Instruction in writing for media that's also standards aligned can thus present a best-of-both-worlds scenario: maximum engagement in generating authentic texts without any sacrifice of rigor.

To this end, CCSS objectives are correlated at the start of every chapter to that chapter's *major* instructional objectives as identified by the special Skills Focus sections. In addition, there are many additional standards-informed skills and concepts addressed throughout the book; these occur both in focused discussions of the writing process and in numerous boxed features—they simply are not *explicitly* called out as such because that would make the correlations too unwieldy. Again, please refer to the index for any specific teachable content in the English language arts.

In practical terms, you might first consider the writing modes and products you need to teach, and then decide which ones could benefit from the fresh approach of media-based writing. Many 10th-grade classes teach material that is a natural, but barely distinguishable, outgrowth from 9th-grade material. Likewise, by the time students hit 11th or 12th grade, they may be revisiting, say, research papers and the requisite skills with roughly the same writing purposes that they've used for several years. The only difference may be one or two new types of sources or the expectation of greater sophistication and/or length in their final drafts. But what could help energize researching more than writing scripts for an original video that, in its informational or persuasive content, is really a documentary (Chapter 5)?

Moreover, what could make the entire process more *authentic* than scripting a media product that can then be produced and even disseminated to the public? Again, although few students may be excited about reading or writing a "research paper" per se, many will want to check out—or help produce—a brief **public service announcement (PSA)** that relies on the same skills for its creation. With this approach in mind, think about whether replacing one or more of your perennial but overworked writing products with scriptwriting might make the task of composition more compelling for your students. The notion of writing for authentic audiences and purposes has benefits that are hard to deny (Routman, 2000), and when we extend the potential audience beyond the school, additional motivational benefits ensue (Slagle, 1997).

Another powerful way to integrate writing for media into your curriculum without feeling that it will lead to some form of upheaval is to revisit the cross-curricular projects that you typically take on as a class. Most English Language Arts teachers welcome opportunities to team-teach with colleagues from other departments, especially since the importance of reading and writing in the content areas has received greater recognition in recent years. By considering audiovisual elements in their writing, students become motivated—not just to write about science or social studies topics, but to make those topics vividly come to life by including media elements drawn from real life. The Literacy

Across the Disciplines feature is therefore included in every chapter to highlight the cross-curricular possibilities of various scriptwriting projects.

Finally, consider that scriptwriting naturally lends itself to collaboration. After all, think about all the times you've seen multiple writers listed in the credits for a film or TV episode. So if you're looking for ways in which your curriculum can be skewed away from the traditional one-text-one-author model, scriptwriting represents a welcome alternative. You can facilitate the creation of student partnerships based upon writing strengths, and be confident that such team-ups reflect how professionals often go about crafting their scripts.

Navigating the Content

As you may already have surmised, individual chapters provide instructional content on media forms that require similar scripts and, therefore, similar writing skills. Within each chapter, points of commonality are covered regarding these closely related script types (e.g., radio drama and news podcasts), and detailed information on each discrete kind of script (i.e., its audience, purpose, and conventions) is also provided.

To use the language of media production, Chapters 1 and 6 are meant to serve as "**intros**" and "**outros**" to the main content of the book—Chapter 1 provides a starting point, covering general strategies and issues related to scripts, and Chapter 6 offers robust extension activities. Therefore, neither chapter includes detailed instruction on the writing process. However, Appendixes B and C, respectively, do include a generic revision checklist and a generic scriptwriting rubric that can be used to support the projects in those chapters, as well as any other script that you and your students decide to tackle.

Each chapter also includes the following standard features, all designed to help you add scriptwriting seamlessly to your lesson and curriculum planning:

- The Why Teach This? feature provides front-ended information that explains why students will love the respective topics and why you'd want to teach them—essentially, engagement and rationale. You can scan these sections to decide whether you'd like to pursue teaching any given type of script.
- The Getting Started section supplies both an overview of the topic and some practical ideas to launch your teaching. In keeping with the book's motivational theme, its QuickStart activities allow you to hit the ground running. Since scriptwriting is often a new topic for students, it's easy to get bogged down in lecturing and explaining. The QuickStarts enable you to introduce concepts inductively and experientially.
- The Make the Connection boxes, also a component of the Getting Started sections (except in Chapter 1, which is *all* about making connections), provide a way for teachers to link that chapter to others or to students' prior experience with scriptwriting and media. The Wrap-Up that concludes every

chapter similarly pulls back to describe and summarize how that chapter's content relates to scriptwriting generally and to broader areas of writing and literacy.

- Nomenclature can be a barrier to learning anything new, but the medium-specific Learn the Lingo feature is designed to be shared with students; it gets them excited about learning how to write new types of scripts by making them feel like "pros." The final piece in Getting Started, this section is key in helping your students make a painless transition to an unfamiliar form of writing. In fact, Learn the Lingo is not simply a local reference resource to be used as needed–many crucial concepts are presented there (and sometimes nowhere else) so that the main text can focus on instruction. That's why this section should be considered one of the central teaching tools of each chapter and therefore less "optional" than others. However, if at any point you need a definition of a script or media term without a full explanation of how it could be used in your projects, you can simply turn to the Glossary of Scriptwriting and Media Terms (Appendix D). In addition, glossary terms are boldfaced throughout the book at point of first use for ease of reference.

- The Script Types section introduces the subtopics of each chapter, distinguishing them from each other before presenting in-depth information on teaching and writing each type separately. (The only reason Chapter 6 does not include this section is that the entire chapter is structured around providing a potpourri of various script types.)

- In terms of pedagogy, it is better for students to first grasp the formal aspects of a given medium and to begin thinking about the challenges and rewards of scripting for it before explicitly learning its particular script format. That's why the Making Friends with the Format section (Chapters 1–5) appears later in each chapter–format can be daunting and should therefore be taught as more of an immediate precursor to writing. Featuring an annotated sample script, this section can be distributed to students both for group instruction and for individual reference when the writing process commences. (Please note that, because of the annotations, the format as shown is not always perfect.)

- The Skills Focus topics in each chapter make an explicit connection between scriptwriting and major aspects of the writing curriculum. Since these are called out in the Table of Contents you can select a specific medium or script format by first deciding which major skills would profit from a new approach in your classroom. A Skills Preview in each chapter highlights additional skills that are covered.

- Literacy Across the Disciplines provides opportunities to link scriptwriting to social studies/history, science, and technology per the general approach of the Common Core State Standards. This section essentially provides a family of cross-curricular applications that you and students can consider just prior to beginning the writing process and choosing a topic.

- The lengthy Writing Process section that crowns each chapter is geared toward a given medium and its accompanying script types in the broadest possible sense. The tips and suggestions here will help you coach students from prewriting through revising in ways that are based upon the relevant parameters and conventions.
- Special Differentiated Instruction boxes appear within the Writing Process sections and address the needs and opportunities that exist for your English Language Learners as well as below-level and advanced students. With this in mind, you might want to peruse this recurring feature in order to select a scriptwriting product that serves a specific student population.

Additional Resources and Assessment

There are tons of scriptwriting resources out there, but they do not often enjoy the visibility with English Language Arts teachers that resources for other forms of writing do. For this reason, *The Power of Scriptwriting!* recommends various programs and reference works in Appendix A.

Also, you might be wondering how to assess all this new script content that students will be writing. To that end, reproducible scriptwriting checklists and rubrics are included in Appendixes B and C.

A Note on Producing Scripts

I won't say that student production of media is not covered here because it's a suitable topic for another book—that's because it's actually a suitable topic for *several* other books. However, you'll see that production ideas are included throughout the book because to avoid the issue altogether is to deny that scripts are a form of practical writing—the question of production can't be put off entirely or just dealt with as an abstraction, and certainly the more students know about media production and the more media literate they are generally, the greater the prior knowledge that they can bring to their writing for any particular medium.

In addition, as a rule of thumb, the book advocates implementing projects that lead to the creation of scripts that students actually have a chance of producing, a practice that makes writing more authentic from the get-go. That's not to say for a movie script project that you want to discourage a couple of 8th-graders who have their heart set on writing a time-travel story in which Vikings and pirates battle each other as they ride on the backs of dinosaurs. But generally you'll want to encourage students to pick topics and a scope that are appropriate so that their projects *could* be made.

There's one more reason why you'll want to tip your hat at least to the notion of production. In the real world, scripts are frequently considered works-in-progress right up until the moment when they are actually performed, drawn, or recorded. In other words, the revision process continues through the production phase itself, as improvements or adjustments are made that could suggest themselves only after collaborators have had a chance to review what the *writers* consider their final draft. Even writers working by themselves on, say, digital stories, may have a last-minute change of heart when placing photos or artwork in sequence as a heretofore unused image sparks a brand-new thought that they can slip into the existing flow of ideas. (For this reason, some media and technology teachers can downplay the role of formal scripts in contrast to this book's approach: They see them as such practical texts that there's no real reason, or time, to dwell on "writing skills" when prewriting or drafting.)

Yet although a voice actor or animator may come up with quite valuable tweaks to any given script, for classroom purposes we will focus mostly on a process wherein scriptwriters must create their own texts with minimal input from others, especially at the early stages. For this reason, as just one example, the chapter on comics will address the full-script (or "DC-style" script, after DC Comics, the publisher of Batman and Wonder Woman) process, in which a writer specifies artwork in advance rather than working side-by-side with the artist every step of the way; there's nothing wrong with the latter approach, which is used by countless professionals, but it's probably best, pedagogically, that students *first* learn how to craft scripts all by themselves before giving up some of their creative autonomy.

WHY SCRIPTS ARE SIMPLER THAN YOU THINK

Finally, a gentle word of caution: Please don't get hung up on formats; writers quickly make the necessary adjustments—remember, the formats are designed to make things easier for writers and readers—and soon become adept at pouring their work into them. The critical idea that organizes this book and gives it a reason for bundling all the topics it does is that once a student—or any writer, really—develops a comfort level with one particular script format, the others are easy to pick up. If you start with comics or a radio play, for example, learning how to script a short film is not too much of a stretch.

Rather than leave this idea at the level of abstraction, however, the Make the Connection notes mentioned earlier highlight specific concepts and skills that exploit the inherent kinship that these seemingly diverse scripts share. This natural coherence of the topic means that you can also do things like start with one assignment working within one type of project medium and then have students work across media in different iterations. For example, a voice-only audio script can later be adapted into a comic, a video, or even a digital story with more than one narrator.

The big takeaway, then, is that scripts are just not that tricky. And the model scripts provided throughout this book bring this point home. Flip through them, check out the annotated script examples in the Making Friends with the Format sections, and you'll discover that writing scripts is not nearly as challenging in terms of format as you might think. In fact, all scripts have the same basic traits:

- They identify who is speaking or a source of sound.
- They describe things either through images or sound that evokes imagery.
- They provide information and directions for cast and crew.

That's it.

So in the end, it's really all about composition and storytelling–the things you already teach. All this book does is demystify scripts and scriptwriting while connecting them to the high-interest media that students already love. And if, as educators, we can do that, then we'll have gone a long way toward demystifying the act of writing itself.

ACKNOWLEDGMENTS

The author extends his gratitude to the following individuals for graciously reading an early draft of select chapters of the manuscript and providing valuable feedback: John Warren, Jeff Share, Katie Monnin, William Kist, and (especially) Frank W. Baker.

CHAPTER 1

CONNECTING STAGE TO SCREEN

If you've read the Introduction, it's likely your mind is more at ease with the notion of writing scripts; the purpose of this chapter is to present various strategies by which you can make your students feel the same way. For example, you probably have some sense of how reading scripts can not only be fun but also function as a fascinating window into the world of many creative media. Likewise, the instruction in this chapter, which connects the "known" practices of reading and writing dramatic plays to the newer practice of doing the same in regard to other scripts, shows students how school-acquired literacies can further their appreciation of the screen-based texts that already appeal to them.

WHY TEACH THIS?

Why do dramatic works for the stage enjoy such prestige in the English language arts curriculum while scriptwriting struggles to find a place at the table? First off, there's the obvious reason: the sheer number of enduring, acknowledged drama classics from across world literature. In fact, we're so used to seeing such texts in canon anthologies and leather-bound treasuries that it's easy to lose sight of the fact that they were not meant to be consumed by the reading public in this manner. To be blunt about it, we view scripts for stage plays as alternate forms of prose narratives rather than what they were originally intended for: to provide sets of instructions for actors, directors, set decorators, and so on.

What's also easy to forget is that even such revered works as those scripts of Shakespearean or classical theater were blueprints for popular entertainment. Many scripts in other media represent contemporary classics of drama or comedy, but they are not designed to be performed by other groups of artists and so their textual nature remains largely hidden from public view: No group decides to put on its own production of *Lawrence of Arabia* or *Finding Nemo*.

Moreover, the collaborative, screen-based, and technology-based nature of much scripted media is precisely the reason why scriptwriting is apt to resonate with today's students. As such, scriptwriting helps fulfill the goals of the "21st-century skills" movement, which has sought to extend literacy instruction beyond print-only texts. Indeed, Dr. Heidi Hayes Jacobs has prominently identified **screenplays, teleplays,** podcasts, **trailers,** and documentaries—all topics covered in this book—as ways to upgrade learner engagement in her "A New Essential Curriculum for a New Time" (H. H. Jacobs, 2010).

However, the common ground that theatrical scripts share with their more recent cousins far outweighs the differences. Ask any secondary teacher, and perhaps most students, to identify the formal features that set a stage play apart from other texts, and you are likely to hear that a stage play does the following:

- Includes detailed directions for movement
- Provides instructions for visual artists and technicians
- Presents dialogue in an easy-to-read format that also includes, as needed, directions for how that dialogue should be delivered
- Is ultimately meant to be performed in order to reach its largest audience
- Contains timeless themes that can be found in other works of literature
- Is generally not intended by the author to be read as a stand-alone text, such as a short story

Clearly, all of the above also applies to scripts in general—not every single script, of course, but certainly to the exemplary ones. All that's needed is a translation of some of the terms. That is, a comic book or animated short might not have "performers" per se, but it does have people (e.g., artists, designers) who need to actualize the script's ideas and bring them to life for audiences.

Similarly, you may be well aware that the traditional stage play represents a kind of textual antecedent for most script types simply by virtue of the fact that it predates the 20th- and 21st-century media with which the rest of the book is concerned. Here's your chance to demonstrate this fact to students and, in the process, show them that scripts aren't really that strange and exotic after all.

Common Core State Standards for Skills Focus

W.7.2. Write informative/explanatory texts to examine a topic and convey ideas, concepts, and information through the selection, organization, and analysis of relevant content.

W.7.4. Produce clear and coherent writing in which the development, organization, and style are appropriate to task, purpose, and audience.

W.11–12.2. Write informative/explanatory texts to examine and convey complex ideas, concepts, and information clearly and accurately through the effective selection, organization, and analysis of content.

W.11–12.4. Produce clear and coherent writing in which the development, organization, and style are appropriate to task, purpose, and audience. (NGA Center & CCSSO, 2010, pp. 42–46)

Skills Preview

In this chapter, you'll learn to help students do the following:

- Practice their critical thinking and transliteracy skills as they compare a script to the media product it led to
- Understand the basic components of all scripts by reviewing what they already know about stage plays
- Adapt an anecdote or personal narrative into a scripted monologue
- Apply the practical writing traits of concision, organization, precision, and audience consideration to a script they compose—and so come to see that all scripts are a form of practical writing
- Sharpen their skills of considering audience and purpose by grasping the concept that scripts in fact have *two* audiences, not just one

GETTING STARTED

This entire chapter is, in a sense, a Getting Started for the book itself; that's why you'll find no detailed suggestions for the writing process: The idea is to build on the familiarity of dramatic scripts, a rather standard part of the English Language Arts curriculum. Similarly, the Making Friends with the Format section in this chapter differs from that in others because you probably don't need an explanation of a stage play's format. In fact, you may want to use your drama unit as a springboard to introduce other forms of media-based writing. As part of such an approach, consider simply asking students why scriptwriting isn't taught much or to speculate about which aspects of stage plays might be shared by screenplays and teleplays, perhaps underlining the word segment *plays*. A discussion that activates prior knowledge—*who has read screenplays or comic book scripts, or written scripts for digital stories?*—can help underscore points of commonality and differentiation. You might even want to capture these in a graphic organizer to which the whole class contributes.

QuickStart: Stand-Up Comedy

To immerse students in the fun, and skills, involved in scriptwriting, have them spend 5 minutes drafting a brief joke in script form that a classmate can then follow to tell that joke either in a small-group or whole-class setting. This can be a joke that students have seen performed, learned from a friend or family member and told themselves, or just made up. Using any play that you have read as a class as a model, students should include pertinent stage directions and parenthetical delivery directions—for example, "whispering" or "screaming". If time permits, have students contrast the actual telling of the joke with its presentation in script form. What worked and what didn't? How might the script be revised to generate more laughs?

Learn the Lingo

act: A substantial dramatic section of a stage play, screenplay, or teleplay. Stage plays can be as brief as one act but typically run to three or more, separated from each other by intermissions or other breaks. A screenplay for a Hollywood movie almost always has exactly three acts, though there is no discernible break in the action. Teleplays for an hour-long TV drama can have as many as five acts–the audience is usually aware of them because commercials separate them.

beat: A parenthetical delivery direction used to signal a very brief pause in plays, teleplays, and screenplays, such as when the audience is to notice that something suddenly occurs to a character. "Pauses," which are longer, are these days more commonly used in theater, while "beats" are used more in screenplays and teleplays.

blocking: Process of planning where actors will stand and move in relation to each other and objects on stage (in a theatrical performance) or on the set (when shooting a movie or TV show). Scriptwriters should know that directors handle the blocking, and so only dramatically important movements should be included in the script.

downstage: The side of a theater's stage that is nearest the audience.

heading: Text used to indicate the beginning of a new scene or act, sometimes called a "scene heading." Although these appear in all caps in scripts across media, for screenplays and teleplays they are formatted flush left and called **"sluglines,"** while in stage play scripts they are centered on the page.

off: When appearing parenthetically next to a character's name, it signals that the following dialogue should be spoken "offstage"; for screen media the equivalent is *O.S.,* for "off-screen," and in comics the same effect is achieved via *O.P.* (**"off-panel"**).

scene: In stage plays, teleplays, and screenplays, dramatic action that occurs within a single place and time period–if the location changes or there is a discontinuous jump backward or forward in time, then one scene has ended and another has begun. Scenes are the structural units that make up an act.

stage left: Positional directions for a theatrical cast and crew. As with *stage right,* the perspective is that of the actors; stage left is thus to the audience's right.

stage right: Positional directions for a theatrical cast and crew. As with *stage left,* the perspective is that of the actors; stage right is thus to the audience's left.

upstage: The side of a theater's stage that is farthest from the audience; "upstaging" was so called because in olden days the stage itself would slope, so that actors could take higher ground relative to their cast mates and thus subtly command the audience's attention.

TEACHING A DRAMATIC SCRIPT TYPE:
PERSONAL NARRATIVE MONOLOGUE

Dramatic scripts have achieved remarkable standardization over the years, so there is little need to draw attention to variations among them; even scripts for puppet theater performances resemble the plays with which students will be familiar. However, you may find it useful to contrast scripts for theatrical monologues with well-known monologues from movies (*The Great Dictator, Saving Private Ryan, On the Waterfront,* and *The Grapes of Wrath* all provide notable examples). Would the latter work if performed live on a stage? Why or why not? Most important, what aspects of the writing, including formatting conventions, help each type of dramatic script fit its particular medium?

Monologues represent an effective way to introduce a variety of script formats, and they can be used to enhance the kind of writing assignments you probably already tackle. As a starting point, simply have students turn a personal anecdote or a first-person narrative into a scripted monologue (or, if you'd like students to write in the practical rather than the narrative mode, skip ahead to the section on informational monologues later in this chapter). Point out that many, if not most, professional monologists share personal narratives (e.g., Garrison Keillor, Spalding Gray), and if you have time you may want to screen clips or play recordings of these as models.

Unlike many other scripts, monologues have the advantage of being able to move directly to "actualization" without a lot of extra prep time or resources. However, keep in mind that when students compose monologues, they often write them as straight prose paragraphs that they then memorize or simply read aloud. Take this opportunity to introduce scriptwriting to your students and to do so in a way that builds on their prior knowledge of playwriting *and* replaces a mere "oral presentation" with something more performative (and therefore supplements conventional composition with a more challenging writing task). Here are some ways to help students take that first-person text and effectively convert it into a script:

1. Have students work with partners or in small groups to provide feedback on each other's read-aloud of the text.
2. Feedback can be verbal, or peer editors can take notes, jotting down directions and suggestions that they then submit to the writer—this helps students practice using specialized vocabulary and dramatic concepts that they can bring to their own work. In fact, you can even have the members of this peer audience role-play the parts of stage directors or casting directors at an audition or rehearsal.
3. Writers can also debrief with their partners or groups, reflecting on both the text and their performance/reading of it. What worked "on the page" but not "live"? What are some elements that they'd like to underscore or eliminate?

4. To enhance students' self-reflection on their work, record the monologues so that they can be played back. What are highlights to be emphasized and weak points to be tweaked or omitted? In this way, performance becomes a tool in the revision/writing process. (Other good tools for this stage of the process might be the generic revision checklist and the generic scriptwriting rubric, which can be found in Appendixes B and C, respectively)

5. Guide students to translate their monologues into stage scripts by incorporating effective stage directions and **line** readings that resulted from steps 1–4, and generally underscoring the text's dramatic moments. Review the terms in Learn the Lingo as needed, and provide text models of stage plays as needed. (Here's a good online source for classic public domain plays that you are free to print and distribute: http://www.one-act-plays.com/royalty_free_plays.html.)

6. Have students rehearse and ultimately perform the new scripted versions of their monologues. Ask partners or groups how both the content and presentation have changed as a result of the scriptwriting and rehearsal processes.

By using this method, students will come to experience what it's like to use the "instructions" in any script in a firsthand way (see the skills section that follows on practical writing). To further enhance these benefits, have students perform *each other's* scripted monologues, just as they did if you opted to try the QuickStart. That way, the performers can work with the authors, and the latter can assess how well their scripts actually function as directions for others to follow.

Finally, the nice thing about a scripted monologue is that it can be incorporated, excerpted, or repurposed into a longer form of a script—it can serve as the voice-over for a digital story, a brief segment within a short film, or even drawn and presented as a mini-comic.

MAKING FRIENDS WITH THE FORMAT: CONDUCT A GUIDED VIEWING

Although this chapter does not deal specifically with writing for the movies or television, there's probably no better way to hook students on scripts—and to engage the multiple literacies involved in understanding and writing them—than to compare a section of a screenplay or teleplay with the corresponding clip that became the end result. In fact, the "guided reading" style routine (Fountas & Pinnell, 1996) that follows would work as an entry point to *any* of the script types covered in the book: It gets students used to reading scripts, and it makes the connection to popular media explicit.

For an example of annotated screenplay with some of the industry jargon explained, please refer to Chapter 4. Of course, as you'll soon see, many of the terms will explain themselves when the print text is compared to the screen text, so try to use a script excerpt that matches the finished project in terms of conventions used (i.e., the dialogue can be slightly different, but if the screenplay calls for an **insert** or an **establishing shot**, the movie scene probably should as well in order to illustrate the concept).

But where to find scripts for classroom use? Although a school librarian or media specialist might be worth consulting on this question, you can also see Scripts for Classroom Use in the Additional Resources section (Appendix A). From the film of your choice, select a clip between 30 seconds and 2 minutes in length, and provide a quick verbal plot summary to provide a context. I recommend that you first show the clip and then move to the print text—many students need to be "oriented" by the visual medium first, while others will simply find it hard to focus on text when the prospect of seeing part of a movie clip is dangled in front of them.

After screening the clip, distribute copies of the corresponding script pages and preview them by having students identify character names, scene headings that indicate setting, and other major elements that will be familiar from their viewing. Then screen the clip again, encouraging students to follow along in the scripts with their fingers. This way, if some have trouble keeping up or lose their way, they can glance over at their classmates to get a general idea of how far along they are in the script.

Now have students mark the script, using checkmarks or exclamation points to highlight sections they like, *x*'s to mark those they dislike, and question marks to note passages or conventions that are confusing. The goal is to show how a script becomes "translated" into the media products with which students are already familiar. This guided script-to-screen process both makes the reading of the script itself more active and can provide the basis for a more in-depth follow-up discussion that prompts critical thinking.

The following questions can be used not only in conjunction with the Guided Viewing activity but also with *any* of the script formats and media types covered in this book. They simply provide a structure so that students can reflect on the particular medium they experience and track its origins back to a print text that they themselves are fully capable of writing. You can watch a news clip, listen to a podcast or radio drama, or perhaps project a couple of pages of a graphic novel onto a classroom screen. All you need are copies of the script that can be compared to and contrasted with the finished product by means of an inquiry similar to what follows.

Pre-Reading/Pre-Viewing Questions:

- What do you already know about the graphic novel/TV show/radio drama/media product?
- Who wrote the script that we're reading?

- Does his or her name appear anywhere on the media product? Does anyone else's? What might that indicate?
- What stage of development does the script represent? Do you think it might have been revised very much after this stage? Why or why not?

"Hit the Pause Button" Questions:

- Where are we on the page?
- Scan ahead in the text. What do you think will happen next?
- What just happened? Summarize the action that you just saw/heard.
- What has happened so far that's different from the script?

Post-Reading/Post-Viewing Questions:

- What content was unexpectedly missing from either the media product or the script that *was* present in the other? What do you think might account for this discrepancy?
- What content was more, or less, successful in the media product than you expected it to be from reading the script?
- How do the script text and the finished media differ in terms of tone or emphasis?
- Do you think the scriptwriter envisioned that the final product would turn out like this?
- How is the script different from other texts you've read? Is it easier or harder to read than, say, a short story or an expository essay on the same general topic or theme? What factors affected your answer?
- How might other scripts (or types of scripts) be different from this one?
- From playing/viewing the media beforehand, what terminology or formatting convention in the script could you figure out?
- Why do you think that particular element of the text is indicated in that manner in the script? Why, and to whom, is the information conveyed by that text important?

SKILLS FOCUS: PRACTICAL WRITING

Using scripted monologues (or really, plays in any form) as the basis for a performance or dramatic reading will give you a sense of how scriptwriting can become one of your most powerful tools in teaching practical writing. It's easy to view scripts primarily as writing products of the creative or expository modes as their purpose is usually to entertain or inform. However, *all* scripts are first and foremost a form of practical writing: They are a set of usable instructions that, most often, someone else will read to create, construct, or perform a media message.

Four Key Traits of Practical Writing

As such, scripts require text that is streamlined and easy to follow—in fact, those are the *only* characteristics that a good scriptwriting "style" needs to have. So, when guiding students through the scriptwriting activities in the pages that follow, bear in mind the traits of concision, organization, precision, and audience in order to turn every script project into an exercise in practical writing. (Because these hallmarks of practical writing provide a common basis for evaluating all scripts, you'll see them mentioned in the writing rubrics in Appendix C.)

Concision. Being concise is important to high-quality writing in most contexts. However, in scriptwriting it's even more crucial because those who read the script as a practical text need to quickly and easily absorb the information that's necessary for their jobs: They don't have time to sift through extensive verbiage or purple prose.

In addition, scripts are often expected to reflect the length of the finished piece—a ten-page script for a 30-second public service announcement (PSA) would be disproportionate. Also, in industries such as film and television, there's a rule of thumb that states that one page of text equals roughly 1 minute of screentime. Therefore, extraneous information prevents scriptwriters' reader-collaborators from getting a true sense of the runtime of the final product.

Organization. The proper ordering of information in a script means *everything*. If readers don't encounter text and ideas in an order that makes sense to them, it really won't matter how good the content is. As in plays, the events and ideas in a script are presented sequentially in a way that corresponds to the order in which audiences will experience them. A narrative script's organization is usually chronological, but not necessarily: Flashbacks and flash-forwards are quite common—adept scriptwriters know how to use them effectively, while beginning scriptwriters simply have fun with them. However, there is no set order for how a script might be produced, and artists and directors can skip around in the text to draw or shoot material as they see fit.

For this reason, scripts present information in ways that follow particular conventions very closely. For example, the data contained in headings (which are sometimes numbered) allow readers to skim and scan scripts to find specific information or scenes quickly and easily. Then, within scenes, descriptions of settings are usually followed by general actions, then precise directions for delivering dialogue, and finally the dialogue itself. Although such an organizational approach to text may seem rigid when compared with prose, it actually provides a much-needed sense of reliability to readers.

Precision. Scriptwriters need to employ an appropriate tone and specific word choice. The latter, in fact, is a form of concision as well—when a young screenwriter knows the term *pan*, for instance, that eliminates the need to describe the camera as "moving in a horizontal way in a continuous shot." And because precise terminology is important, be sure to draw attention to the items in the Learn the Lingo features throughout the book so that you can help your students speak and write like pros. (For vocabulary related to media more generally, or for terms covered in chapters other than the one at hand, simply turn to the Glossary.)

Audience. Just as scriptwriters use special media-related vocabulary, they also pour their text into a specific format that is designed to accommodate the needs of their readers. This audience of potential collaborators needs to be able to glean certain information at a glance. Actors will want to see how many lines they have, producers will want a sense of the locations involved for budgetary reasons, and comic book artists will want to know how much space they have on a given page and how much will be eaten up by dialogue.

It's for this reason that some script formats call out certain words in "all caps" (LIKE THIS) or break text into chunks that feature consistent heads and typography. Overlong sentences or a convoluted structure will, therefore, not only keep readers from enjoying the content as with any type of writing, but will also prevent them from actually being able to produce a script effectively. In a sense this is a major trade-off in all forms of scriptwriting—it offers less of an opportunity to develop an authorial voice, but it provides a constant vehicle to practice trimming words and expressing ideas as efficiently as possible.

Informational Monologues

You can make practical writing the writing mode to spotlight in any given script format. Just have students create a script for an informational monologue that demonstrates the procedural steps in doing something—building a birdhouse, shooting foul shots, baking a dessert. All the products that usually come out of practical texts, such as recipes and how-to essays, can be written as scripts.

First, decide on a format and medium. Will the scripts be for a short video, a comic strip, or a digital story consisting of a series of photos with a voice-over? (The nitty-gritty of all these writing products is covered in the succeeding chapters.) Regardless of script format, coach students to follow the same prewriting processes (e.g., listing and ordering key steps and resources) that they would in any form of practical writing. Then they can think about how their scripts will use the chosen medium most effectively. For example, a script for a TV-style cooking show is a great way to convey information and techniques in ways that print or still images alone are not capable of doing.

Students may wonder, however, about how to go about crafting such a script. In this case, instruct them to conceive of the text as a monologue. Rather than being dramatic, however, this is an "informational" monologue that speaks directly to the viewer while each step in the kitchen is performed. Students can then simply use this script to act out and record such monologues with a video camera or even just a phone. Nothing fancy, in terms of a set, **camera angles**/movements, or transitions, is required. One continuous running of the camera might be all that's needed.

Or, if time and resources permit, students can add **close-up** and cutaway **shots** to their scripts to convey greater detail or perhaps even include an "intro" or "outro" that shows people enjoying the dish. As models of sequence and clarity, you might want to make available some examples of commercially or professionally created informational DVDs on particular topics (e.g., fishing and outdoor skills, computer tutorials, arts and crafts) for students to view and take notes on.

And just to be clear, scripts can be assessed even if they are never performed in this way. Yes, producing them is always a nice option, but it's not necessary for students to reap the full benefits of the assignment. In part that's because all scripts can be evaluated on their consideration of audience and purpose, regardless of whether they are ever actually experienced by an actual audience. After all, that's how producers decide whether they *want* to produce any given script.

SKILLS FOCUS: AUDIENCE AND PURPOSE

Scriptwriting provides a sophisticated, fun, and authentic way to reinforce the concepts of writing for an audience and purpose. That's why the rubrics in Appendix C for *every* script format include these concepts in some form or another—and why it might make sense for you to return to them as touchstones in all your instruction around scriptwriting. (For a validation of the importance of writing with a specific audience and purpose in mind, please see the CCSS correlations at the start of this chapter.)

However, you should keep in mind that the process of considering audience and purpose is more complex in scriptwriting than students have probably encountered elsewhere. In a sense, we've already covered the notion of purpose: *All* scripts have a primary purpose of serving as a set of practical blueprints to create a media product. Their secondary purpose is the one we associate with other texts—to inform, persuade, entertain, and so on.

Similarly, scripts have a primary *and* a secondary audience. The primary audience is everyone who will read it as a practical document in order to produce it. The secondary audience—not secondary in importance but in the order that it experiences the work—is the public that becomes aware of the script through that completed media product.

Typically, in-school writing involves writing for one's teachers, classmates, and occasionally the wider school community through intranets, local bulletin boards, literary magazines, school newspapers, and yearbooks. Sometimes students, often under a teacher's guidance, will submit a piece of writing to an outside contest or publisher. All of that is great.

Scriptwriting, however, affords the opportunity to augment these audiences in ways that are supremely authentic. That's because if students can compose a sufficiently engaging and polished script, there's no reason why they can't follow up and get friends, peers, family members, industry professionals in their community, and others interested in helping them make their scripted project a reality. (Of course, there's always the possibility of students working with classmates, under your direction, to bring that script to life—see the note on producing in the Introduction.) Furthermore, some students may not have the confidence to enter a poem or an essay in a contest—but they may be motivated to enter a script in a contest or create a short video and submit it to a youth-oriented film festival.

Yes, some of this newfound confidence may derive from the collaborative nature of producing scripts—students can team up with peers whose skills and talents complement their own. But a large part of the transformation you may witness in students' attitudes toward writing will stem from their new conception of composition itself. Students with stories to tell but who never considered themselves "writers," because they didn't feel they were adequate wordsmiths in prose, will suddenly be able to tell those stories through images and sound as they craft scripts for videos, comics, or podcasts.

In addition to the practical aspects that the primary audience will look for in a script, the secondary audience has certain expectations from the medium, and it's up to the script to deliver these as well. And this holds true in terms of both the script's genre and the formal aspects of its particular medium. A student-written TV-style commercial, for example, may not be as slick or call for the same production values as a professional version, but there's no reason it can't feature the same standard elements, such as a **tagline** or a product image. Similarly, students may be familiar with static YouTube "videos" that display only a single still image while a song plays on the audio track. To underscore the importance of audience expectations, you can ask students why such a use of the medium might be disappointing for viewers who expect moving images, not simply digital audio.

In the end, satisfying an audience and fulfilling a purpose are the overriding goals that all other writing traits—concision, organization, and precision, to name just a few—exist to serve. In the chapters that follow we'll take a detailed look at how students can develop these traits in their writing as they practice addressing the needs of varied audiences and purposes.

LITERACY ACROSS THE DISCIPLINES: TELLING UNTOLD STORIES

In terms of pop cultural awareness, the term *monologue* brings to mind images of late-night talk show hosts opening their broadcasts. Use this touchstone, and students' familiarity (perhaps gained from this chapter's QuickStart) with stand-up comedy, which is an entire art form premised upon a single performer, to challenge students to script a comedy routine that playfully shows off their knowledge of the content areas. Specifically, have them share the secret stories, or "confessions," behind well-known events or phenomena.

Science topics on this theme might include what a cell feels as it undergoes division, or the guilty admissions of a virus or destructive storm system. An example drawn from social studies would be an irreverent "untold" history, such as what George Washington was *really* feeling as he crossed the Delaware (or what it was like to be the first president in a nation that had no prior experience with presidents). To encourage creativity, explain to students that they need only to create the script for such comedy monologues, not to perform them. In fact, consider having *other* students (or even faculty members) perform the scripts that your class writes.

Regardless of the topics that are chosen, or whether the monologues are even performed, make sure that students understand the importance of using reality-based details in their scripts. This means that elements such as staging and delivery directions for the monologist should not only be humorous but also relate to the content-area specifics in a way that demonstrates an understanding of them.

WRAP-UP

You will probably find that, once having introduced scriptwriting in the contexts of practical writing, reading stage plays, close readings of scripts paired to viewings, or considering audience and purpose, students may do things like the following:

- Watch or listen to more carefully and interrogate more closely *any* media that are presented in class, asking questions such as, "What was actually in the script . . . and what was a creative decision made at a later point?"
- Find motivation to respond to a play by rewriting it as a script for another medium (e.g., What creative possibilities arise if it's converted to a radio drama? How might the tone change if it's adapted into a comic book?).
- Come up with unpredictable, but rich and authentic, topics for practical writing assignments that are informed by other media: how-to videos on YouTube, home repair/decorating texts inspired by cable TV shows, and so on.
- Find new excitement for writing in general as they realize that scriptwriting is a powerful way to connect writing, and all the related skills that you teach, to their personal interests in media and pop culture and thus to their outside-of-school literacies.

CHAPTER 2

Spoken Word and Audio Scripts

The power of the spoken word still captivates. Indeed, many of today's students listen avidly to interest-specific podcast series—or even produce them! Others may recall the pleasure of being read to and how the right spoken text can open up their imaginations. Point out to students that writing audio scripts gives them a way to tap into the magical power of the spoken word themselves.

WHY TEACH THIS?

Love words? Want your students to develop a love of language—an appreciation of both its musicality and its impact on our thinking? Great. Because when students write audio scripts, which arguably exalt the power of words above other script formats, that's exactly what will start to happen. Moreover, the benefits of reading aloud—which audio scripts do in a naturally authentic way (unlike reading novels, which are not intended to be read aloud)—have long been shown to have multiple literacy benefits (Fountas & Pinnell, 1996).

Common Core State Standards for Skills Focus

W.7.2d. Use precise language and domain-specific vocabulary to inform about or explain the topic.

W.7.3d. Use precise words and phrases, relevant descriptive details, and sensory language to capture the action and convey experiences and events.

W.7.6. Use technology, including the Internet, to produce and publish writing and link to and cite sources as well as to interact and collaborate with others, including linking to and citing sources.

SL.7.4. Present claims and findings, emphasizing salient points in a focused, coherent manner with pertinent descriptions, facts, details, and examples; use appropriate eye contact, adequate volume, and clear pronunciation.

SL.7.6. Adapt speech to a variety of contexts and tasks, demonstrating command of formal English when indicated or appropriate.

W.11–12.2d. Use precise language, domain-specific vocabulary, and techniques such as metaphor, simile, and analogy to manage the complexity of the topic.

W.11–12.3d. Use precise words and phrases, telling details, and sensory language to convey a vivid picture of the experiences, events, setting, and/or characters.

W.11–12.6. Use technology, including the Internet, to produce, publish, and update individual or shared writing products in response to ongoing feedback, including new arguments or information.

SL.11–12.4. Present information, findings, and supporting evidence, conveying a clear and distinct perspective, such that listeners can follow the line of reasoning, alternative or opposing perspectives are addressed, and the organization, development, substance, and style are appropriate to purpose, audience, and a range of formal and informal tasks.

SL.11–12.6. Adapt speech to a variety of contexts and tasks, demonstrating a command of formal English when indicated or appropriate. (NGA Center & CCSSO, 2010, pp. 42–46)

Skills Preview

In this chapter, you'll learn to help students do the following:

- Develop characters psychologically by using the unique properties of audio
- Create and sustain mood with strategies drawn from classic radio drama
- Engage in a series of activities involving word choice, including the creation of a "verbal thesaurus" geared to the spoken word
- Practice their speaking and listening skills in engaging and authentic ways

GETTING STARTED

In a world where video games are ubiquitous and all the new movies are released in 3-D, media products that rely on audio alone may strike some students as lacking in, um, sensory stimulation. Of course that's before you point out to them that they're probably fans of some form of music, aren't they?

While you're at it, you might want to explain that sound is often the trigger for a wide range of emotions and sensations within their favorite media products. To illustrate this, invite students to name their favorite soundtracks to pop culture works, and then dig deeper—discuss the ways that audio elements accent the humor or excitement of video games, cite examples of theme songs and musical motifs that enhance the TV shows they're fans of, or show how sound effects in movies—the howling wind or the roars of alien monsters—can immerse audiences more completely in fictional worlds.

QuickStart: Traffic and Weather Updates

Here's a way to get your students into audio scripts quickly, intuitively, and with little or no technology. Using a classroom board or flipchart, write speaker identifiers in the following order, creating a group template—or several of them in order to engage multiple small groups:

Anchor: _____

Weather reporter: _____

Anchor: _____

Traffic reporter: _____

Anchor: _____

Start by asking students to share what they know about traffic and weather updates that are broadcast over radio, making sure that they understand that these are brief informational **segments**. Then explain that they will write 5- to 15-second texts for three parts: **anchor**, weather reporter, and traffic reporter. The anchor should introduce each reporter, who in turn gives updates about current conditions.

For a weather update, students can simply look out the window, or paraphrase weather forecasts they've heard in the past day or so. For a traffic update, they can draw upon conditions that morning on the way to school—or, if you have more time, you can incorporate a technology component by having an outside partner (a parent or faculty member) text or phone in real-time conditions. The point is to get kids writing ASAP: Assign parts, do a quick read-through of the text and revise as necessary, and then do a final read-through. Students can rotate through the reading and writing roles. You can also add embellishments, such as "Today's Traffic Update is brought to you by _____ (your class name? a local business?)."

The skills to concentrate on in this activity are the clarity and brevity of information, the transition of the anchor ("Next, we'll turn to _____"), and, most of all, the way students work as a team under time-sensitive conditions so that they can practice the art of prewriting on the fly as journalists do. The challenge is to gather information, organize it, write a rough script under stopwatch conditions ("Can you do this in under 180 seconds?"), practice reading it, revise it as necessary, and then "publish" it by reading it aloud to the class—all in about 10 minutes.

QuickStart—A Variation: Audio and Setting

For a variation on this QuickStart activity, or similar projects that require specific locations, consider assigning more unusual settings. For example, it might be fun to allow students to choose different locations for the weather or traffic reports: London, Antarctica, the summit of Mount Everest, under the ocean, and so on. By applying the same concepts to different places, students will begin to see how the construction of their messages changes when the context changes. In London, the script would call for the anchor and reporters to speak with a British accent, while a script for a mountaintop setting should include the sound effect of blowing wind. Use this approach to help students appreciate the distinct aspects of different settings, perhaps even basing an audio script on a setting from a novel or short story that you've read as a class.

Make the Connection: The Persuasive Power of Sound

To convey the importance of sound in media, use a classroom activity that Frank Baker of the online Media Literacy Clearinghouse has told me he advocates in his professional-development sessions. Simply play a recorded TV commercial for students—after first instructing them to close their eyes and listen carefully. Once playback is complete, ask students to make a list of everything they've heard. The goal is to increase their awareness of the often underappreciated role that sound plays in our visually oriented culture.

Have students share what they've heard in the commercial; analyze how each sound contributed to the overall message, especially in terms of its persuasive power. Then play the commercial a second time, now letting students watch it as you point out any sounds that they may have missed or misidentified. I even suggest you play the commercial a third time as you prompt students to identify each sound by its *type* of audio element. Is it simply spoken word audio, as in dialogue or narration, or does it belong to one of the categories described in the Recorded Poetry section of this chapter?

Baker originally conceived of this as part of an introduction to two-column video scripts, which means that you can also use this activity with the projects in Chapter 5. However, its emphasis on sound makes it ideal for getting things off the ground with audio scripts.

Learn the Lingo

break/interlude: An announcement or stand-alone musical piece that serves as a break between segments.

contact info: Where the producers of the podcast can be reached by listeners with questions; an e-mail address should be sufficient. Student podcasters should consider opening a dedicated email account in the show's name rather than making their personal information public.

cue: The signal for a type of audio in a radio drama script.

dead air: An extended period without any sound at all.

fade in/fade out: Denotes audio that is gradually increasing or decreasing in volume; often appears as a transitional device. Note that "fade in/out" is also used in film in reference to the visibility of a screen image.

flashback: In any narrative medium and genre, a leap backward in the story's chronology before resuming in its normal direction.

flash-forward: In any narrative medium and genre, a leap forward in the story's chronology. To spark audience interest, some scriptwriters begin with a flash-forward in the form of a prologue.

ID: Brief reminder to listeners of the show or station they're listening to. These are arguably not as necessary for podcasts as they are for traditional radio since listeners to the former do not switch as randomly or abruptly between shows/channels.

intro: Short for "introduction"; lines spoken by a host or narrator to set up a given segment or to open a podcast.

line: As in a stage play, this term refers to spoken text, not directions or cues.

MP3: The format most popular for sharing digital music files.

music bed: Music over which speech or other audio is heard.

off-mike/off-mic: A delivery direction that indicates that a line should sound distant, mumbled, or otherwise indistinct to the listener. Lines that are delivered off-mike can add a touch of realism or mystery to an audio production, or just provide a sense of space surrounding the central action.

outro: The opposite of an intro; a wrap-up of an individual segment.

podcast: Downloadable audio or video files than can be played on computers or, commonly, on mobile playing devices such as Apple's iPod.

PSA: Short for "Public Service Announcement," a brief informational/persuasive message that is provided for the good of the listening public.

segment: A small section of a podcast episode, usually focusing on a given topic or theme (the term is used in television broadcasting as well). Student podcasting teams may want to rotate between writing, producing, and on-air duties on a segment-by-segment basis in order to familiarize themselves with the demands and challenges of each role.

sound bite: A brief audio excerpt of a longer recording; these can be incorporated into what is otherwise a scripted piece, as in a news spot.

tagline: A memorable catchphrase or slogan, usually for a media product, publisher, or advertised commodity.

SPOKEN WORD AND AUDIO SCRIPT TYPES

Compared with any other medium considered in this book, scripts for audio probably have the greatest flexibility in terms of formatting and the degree to which writers can experiment and come up with an approach that works for them. Of course common to all spoken word and audio scripts is a basic structure on the page that identifies speakers and other sound sources, and indicates their sequence (or overlap, as the case may be). In that sense they should recall stage play scripts for students, which similarly have an emphasis on dialogue and the spoken word. (In the theater, the creative personnel who use the script have much greater leeway in realizing what the audience sees than those who work in, say, film and comics.) However, as you'll see right away with recorded poetry, one can invent script forms that best wed a given kind of text to the artistic, performative or curricular needs of you and your students. The other script types presented in the following pages, those for radio drama and news/PSAs, conform to industry standards that have evolved over time. Yet even with those types of scripts you have the ability to adapt them to fit into the larger context of a podcast, the final topic covered in this chapter.

Recorded Poetry

Audio scripts represent a natural way to support students' composition of, and response to, poetry, thus connecting writing to the literature curriculum. In fact, they can write scripts that can then be recorded and presented as a podcast series.

But this begs the question, *What does a script of a poetry reading actually look like? Isn't it the text of the poem itself?* The answer is, while it's certainly based upon that text, a script can also specify that the audio production add the following:

Sound effects. Even simple ones can be surprisingly evocative.

Ambient sound. A poem about life in school can be recorded as it's read in the lunchroom or on a playground or athletic field—or even a busy hallway just after the bell has sounded between classes. **Ambient sound** is a highly effective way to convey setting and should reinforce the importance of using similar auditory-based sensory imagery in other forms of writing.

Music. A script can "**spec**" music in a way that's generic in terms of source but still precise for the dramatic or literary needs of the piece. For a Shakespearian sonnet, Renaissance music can be requested—or so can pop music on a similar theme.

Introduction. Readers can include a short passage that explains either the genesis of the poem, if they wrote it, or what inspired them to select it if they did not.

Choral effects. Can others contribute to the recording besides the main reader? This might include having other speakers whisper in the background or participate boisterously in a call-and-response structure.

Audio effects. Adding echoes and other audio devices isn't necessary in a script for recorded poetry, but it can add accents to the text and highlight its rhythms. If you're wondering how "audio effects" differ from "sound effects," audio effects are produced by altering or manipulating already recorded sounds, speech, or music, while sound effects are created (or inserted from an outside source or file) to fit specific purposes. (And if this or other aspects of audio production or podcasting sound way too technical for you, check out Appendix A for some handy and/or free resources that can help.)

A simple but interesting use of recorded verse was developed by Illinois educators Kelly Farrow and Erin Meehan and based upon the Newbery-winning collection *Joyful Noise: Poems for Two Voices* (Fleischman, 1988). Each line of poetry is divided between speakers who alternate (and sometimes overlap) their recitation; the script text still generally flows left-to-right, but if "Voice A" is silent to start a line, you'll notice a blank spot in the script, which means that listeners will hear the text below that blank space first because "Voice B" is speaking alone. (If this sounds confusing, just peek at the sample below—the format is actually pretty intuitive.) After having students write a poem that reads like a musical duet, Farrow and Meehan then have them record a podcast. I, in turn, have adapted their script template to provide the following example, the concluding stanza of Walt Whitman's "Beat! Beat! Drums!" (By the way, other terrific poems that would work in this respect include Robert Frost's "Stopping by Woods on a Snowy Evening" and Lewis Carroll's "Jabberwocky.")

```
Voice A: (loudly) Beat! beat! drums — blow!          blow!
Voice B: (loudly) Beat! beat!          blow! bugles! blow!

Voice A: Make no parley —
Voice B:                    stop for no expostulation,

Voice A: Mind not the timid —
Voice B:                        mind not the weeper or prayer,

Voice A:                        beseeching the young man,
Voice B: Mind not the old man

Voice A: Let not the child's voice be heard,
Voice B:                                nor the mother's entreaties,

Voice A: Make even the trestles to shake the dead
Voice B:                              the dead where they lie awaiting
                                     the hearses,

Voice A: (softly) So strong you thump O terrible drums — so loud you
                  bugles blow.
Voice B: (softly) So strong you thump O terrible drums — so loud you
                  bugles blow.
```

The neat thing about this format is that it is simple to grasp and reproduce. You can share it as a blank template with write-on lines for adding text for two (or more) voices, the voices paired for each line of poetry; you could even add empty parentheses after each voice where students can add delivery directions (e.g., "softly"). Explain to students that text navigation is always left-to-right, even if that means reading the second line in a pair before the first if the second line has text to the left of where the text of the first line begins. In the "Beat! Beat! Drums!" example, "Voice A" is not always the first speaker (e.g., "Mind not the old man") in a given pairing of lines. Also, choral effects become possible, as in the first and final two paired lines of the script, and for the single word *dead* in the penultimate line of the poem, enabling the voices to speak simultaneously for added volume and emphasis. Moreover, the simple, clear structure of the format allows students to discover a text's natural rhythms as they must decide how to divide lines between speakers.

Note, too, that additional voices could be added as well as other audio effects and music. The main point, though, is that scripting recorded poetry doesn't mean simply transcribing a poem in a new format. It means thinking about the poem's natural breaks and emphases: Does it have a recurring refrain that speakers can play with in some way? Or does it already include speakers in dialogue with each other as certain poems by Langston Hughes do? And of course if your students are composing their own poetry, they can write with audio in mind. They might be surprised by the range of creative, evocative possibilities that result.

A Note on Copyright. Professional broadcasters need permission to use non–public domain text (if it's being read aloud) as well as any previously published music. However, be aware that the principle of **Fair Use** (see the additional resources in Appendix A) should protect the use of copyrighted text or music if it's strictly for educational purposes. In general, for audio scripts, you'll want to follow the same guidelines regarding copyrighted material as you would for other media production with students. Of course students who are also musicians might obviate the need for outside music by composing a few measures to establish atmosphere or to be played as the title of a piece is read.

Radio Drama

Radio drama scripts can be used to teach writing in a variety of genres, from comedy to mystery to horror and science fiction. Without exception, though, all these types of radio plays enable young writers to develop the following in their work:

- *Character*. With no visual representation of the main character or characters, the audience more easily identifies with them *psychologically*. That's because we never really have to contend with characters who simply do (or don't) resemble us physically–instead, we are privy to their thoughts and emotions, and this intimacy makes us more deeply responsive to their situations. Radio drama, therefore, combines the immediacy of staged or filmed dramas with the sense of an *interior* world that prose literature provides.

- *Plot.* Radio dramas must move quickly and efficiently. They must establish an inciting incident, throw obstacles in the way of the protagonist, and maintain a level of dramatic tension that makes people want to keep listening. There are no visuals of likable actors or interesting locations to distract or amuse an audience, so the story itself must be involving throughout.
- *Imagery.* Like poetry, radio drama relies on well-chosen words to evoke images in listeners' imaginations. When those words are combined with sound effects and music, they can re-create an entire sensory world for the audience in a way that's both unique and memorable.

Radio dramas can be presented live, as readings on a stage. They can also be recorded, saved to a CD, and distributed to their audience that way. But one of the big reasons the radio drama has made a comeback in recent years is that podcasts can be created for webcasting and archiving, allowing students to reach an audience as wide as the Internet and as close as the phone in their pocket.

Need a classic model of the form? Howard Koch and Anne Froelick's script for Orson Welles's famed 1938 adaptation of *The War of the Worlds* is frequently anthologized in secondary literature textbooks. If you have access to the text, it would be great to use as a model of the elements that make for impactful radio drama. (To see a copy of the script, visit http://www.radioheardhere.com/waroftheworlds/.) As an alternate model for radio drama, both in terms of detailed formatting conventions and as an example of literature adaptation, see this chapter's Making Friends with the Format.

News Broadcasts and Audio PSAs

A news broadcast or public service announcement (PSA) can be aired over the PA system at school, incorporated into a digital production, or uploaded as a podcast to a class or school website or intranet. PSAs are covered in greater depth in Chapter 5 because video PSAs are extremely common as well, and additional information about writing news scripts can also be found in that chapter. Here are some ideas to keep in mind when you and your students tackle these genres purely as audio:

- Student scripts should call for the inclusion of ambient sound whenever it's appropriate and possible. To demonstrate how effective this can be, play an NPR-style news piece and draw attention to how this device so easily suggests a particular setting.
- For a sense of how to organize a news broadcast, revisit this chapter's QuickStart activity for a basic structure that your students can elaborate on: A news anchor introduces and concludes individual segments, which themselves may be scripted to varying degrees.

- Although it may make sense for students to collaborate on scripts and the recording itself, it's entirely possible for audio pieces to be one-person shows. In news segments, for example, the anchor and reporter can be the same person: "[As Anchor] I wanted to find out more about how our school helps the community . . . [As Reporter, with ambient street sounds] so I asked some of the local storekeepers how they benefited from having a school in their neighborhood . . . [this could lead into an unscripted **sound bite**]."
- Audio PSAs should focus on the spoken text, with sound effects and other elements used sparingly, if at all. With PSAs, the goal is to convey information clearly and quickly.
- While prewriting their PSAs, students may discover that they have a wealth of material on their chosen topic. You can suggest that they divide their main points into separate bullet points, each of which can serve as the basis for a series of 15-second PSAs (two or three sentences and then the tagline, a punchy catchphrase) rather than trying to fit everything into a single 30- or 60-second spot.

Podcasts

Strictly speaking, podcasts are not really a distinct kind of audio *production* (and thus requiring their own script style) but rather a *platform* for distributing audio productions digitally. You can create a podcast for a news spot, a radio-style drama, a spoken word performance of poetry, or any other text. You can even create a kind of audio magazine that focuses on each of these types of scripts over different segments.

Indeed, the versatility of podcasts (which can also encompass video files) is one reason they're so popular these days. Another involves the ubiquity of devices like Apple's iPod, from which the podcast derives its name. However, you don't need such devices to listen to, record, or of course script a podcast. Virtually any computer with a web browser, and many mobile devices, can play podcasts, which means that students can upload or e-mail them to reach their intended audience.

To be sure, not every single moment of a podcast needs to be scripted. However, certain sections definitely *should* be, such as the introduction, the wrap-up, announcements, promotions of upcoming shows, and of course, any transitional moments between unscripted sections. Even if a podcast consists only of an interview where the responses are open-ended, students will still need to script their questions and follow-up questions. Here are some other things to think about:

- If they are developing a radio-style podcast, scriptwriters should try to balance the somewhat conflicting goals of providing a crisp, professional-sounding recording and the need to sound fresh and spontaneous to listeners. Coach students to note the proportion of scripted to unscripted portions in their podcasts.

- Point out that the nonlive nature of podcasts allows for flexibility: Students can rescript and rerecord segments that don't work as originally planned before disseminating the final version.
- Scripts should identify the title of a podcast, its date, and, if applicable, its episode number. Remind students that there won't necessarily be any print text for listeners to refer to for this kind of information. Scripts might also include brief credits at the end listing the main writers, readers, or performers.
- Students should focus on writing an attention-grabbing opening or intro. Unlike with visual media, it's easy for people to become distracted while listening to audio since it's possible they are doing other things at the same time. Incorporating high-energy music that can fade into a background sound, or "**music bed**" as it's called in audio production, for spoken text is one way of commanding listener attention.
- Student scriptwriters should strive to keep things brief: The amount of text in a standard five-paragraph essay, for example, might be too long. However, if students feel constrained by the importance placed upon brevity, they can explore the possibility of creating a podcast series rather than a single episode. Then they can cover a given topic over multiple segments.
- In general, you can plan the time needed for writing by first estimating how long it would take students to write the analogous kind (and amount) of text in a more standard format. For example, a news spot might equal one paragraph or one page of expository text, and a PSA might correspond to writing a persuasive essay of the same length. Then factor in the additional time it will take students to translate their ideas, research, and other prewriting into script format—a process that will become increasingly faster the more experience they gain with scripts.

MAKING FRIENDS WITH THE FORMAT

The following sample script is an adaptation of Edgar Allan Poe's "The Cask of Amontillado," and, again, it is somewhat more detailed and modern in terms of format than the one for *The War of the Worlds*. As such, it can serve as an easy-to-use model for creating scripts that your students may eventually want to perform and record. Reproduce it and review the annotations as needed to highlight the key features of radio drama and the audio script format more generally. As I remarked on earlier, notice the similarity to stage plays, particularly in the reliance on dialogue.

The Cask of Amontillado   →2

4. NARRATOR	→(TO AUDIENCE) It was about dusk, one evening during the supreme madness of the carnival season, that I encountered my . . . friend.	Page numbers in scripts should always go at the top (this is the second page because the first would be a title page with the author's name). Also, when actors will be speaking the lines, try to use the font Courier to make reading easy.
5. SOUND	MERRYMAKING CROWD NOISE SWELLS, THEN SUBSIDES	
6. NARRATOR	(TO AUDIENCE) Some may think that →its madness was infectious . . . (WHISPERING) and indeed perhaps it was.	Cues are numbered like this so that people can quickly find specific passages. Some scripts start numbering anew with every scene or page, but that's probably not necessary in a short, student-penned script.
7. SOUND	SUDDEN CACKLE OF LAUGHTER FROM CARNIVAL CELEBRANT ↑	These "delivery directions" are always in all caps and in parentheses so they stand out as "not to be spoken."
8. NARRATOR	(TO AUDIENCE) Fortunato accosted me with excessive warmth, for he had been celebrating much.	
9. FORTUNATO	(ENTERING) Oh, my dear, dear fellow, how goes it with you?	The script creates a connection between an interior state and external events by using a well-timed sound effect to punctuate this psychological blurring.
10. NARRATOR	→(TO AUDIENCE) The man wore motley. He had on a tight-fitting parti-striped dress, and his head was surmounted by the conical cap and bells.	Sometimes this delivery direction is indicated by "(NARRATING)" in a script. Here the narrator has no name, so that might be confusing.
11. SOUND	SMALL BELLS JINGLING PLAYFULLY	
12. NARRATOR	I was so pleased to see him that I thought I should never have done wringing his hand.	
13. NARRATOR	My dear Fortunato, how remarkably well you are looking today! But I have received a pipe of what passes for Amontillado . . .	
14. FORTUNATO	Impossible! And in the middle of the carnival!	
15. NARRATOR	→I have my doubts, and I was silly enough to pay the full Amontillado	Adapting prose stories is often fairly straightforward. Here the original line is "'I have my doubts,' I replied."

NARRATOR/CONT'D OVER

NARRATOR/CONT'D   price without consulting you. You were not to be found, and I was fearful of losing a bargain.

16. FORTUNATO   Amontillado!

17. NARRATOR   I have my doubts.

18. FORTUNATO   Amontillado!

19. NARRATOR   And I must satisfy them.

20. FORTUNATO   Amontillado! Come, let us go.

Radio drama works well with as few speaking parts as possible, as it can be difficult for the audience to distinguish many characters from each other. Note how Poe's quick, back-and-forth dialogue is a good fit for the medium.

21. NARRATOR   Whither?

22. FORTUNATO   To your vaults!

23. NARRATOR   (TO AUDIENCE) Thus speaking, Fortunato possessed himself of my arm, and I suffered him to hurry me to my palazzo.

24. SOUND   CROWD NOISE SWELLS

25. MUSIC   OMINOUS

26. SOUND   JANGLE OF KEYS

Sound effects, dialogue, and music called out on the left like this are called "cues"—at some point during recording or broadcasting, the person responsible for contributing that bit of audio will be cued by the director.

You could insert a "scene head" here similar to those in movies or comics to indicate the change in setting to Fortunato's home. Many older radio dramas do not do this, however.

27. NARRATOR   (TO AUDIENCE) There were no attendants at my home; they had absconded to make merry in honor of the time. (TO FORTUNATO) Here, take a torch so that you might find your way in this gloom.

28. FORTUNATO   (MUTTERING GREEDILY, GIGGLING TO HIMSELF) Amontillado, Amontillado, Amontillado . . .

29. NARRATOR   Yes, my friend, presently. The vaults lie at the foot of this winding staircase.

30. SOUND   FOOTSTEPS DESCENDING AND ECHOING—THEN, A SUDDEN JINGLE OF BELLS AS IF FORTUNATO HAS LOST HIS BALANCE

31. NARRATOR   Fortunato, take care! I would not wish any harm to befall you! (QUIETLY, TO SELF) Not yet at any rate . . .

SKILLS FOCUS: WORD CHOICE

Here's a description of a Martian invader spoken by an eyewitness in a hypothetical radio drama script:

> The mouth is scary-looking and drooling. It has skinny lips that seem to be moving a little.

Now, here's a description of a Martian invader from the script for radio broadcast of *The War of the Worlds*, mentioned earlier:

> The eyes are black and gleam like a serpent. The mouth is V-shaped with saliva dripping from its rimless lips that seem to quiver and pulsate. (Koch & Froelick, 1938)

Use these examples and others of your choosing to illustrate the importance of word choice to students. Point out that thoughtful word selection makes the difference between simply *recording* text and artfully *creating* an immediate and compelling world that listeners enter. Explain that other than sound effects and music, which often play limited roles, everything in an audio script consists of words, and that's why every single one counts so much. Following are some additional points to give to students who are writing audio scripts:

- Recall the difference between connotation and denotation. Cite this chapter's excerpts from *The War of the Worlds* to illustrate how effective scriptwriting is mindful of words' connotative meanings. For example, using the word *serpent* instead of repeating *snake* (see below) conveys a deeper meaning because we associate the word with a grand sense of evil and doom from its biblical usage, not simply a physical description.
- Figurative language such as metaphors helps create mental imagery for listeners. Similes are especially potent. To illustrate this point vividly for students, share this section of *The War of the Worlds* in which the Martians are first described: "Good heavens, something's wriggling out of the shadow like a gray snake. . . . They look like tentacles to me. There, I can see the thing's body. It's large, large as a bear and it glistens like wet leather." (Koch & Froelick, 1938)
- When dialogue features analogies to help listeners picture unusual images by using the familiar to describe the unfamiliar, the effect can also be quite powerful and evocative.
- Effective word choice also means using slang, dialect, and figures of speech to differentiate characters in radio dramas. Since the audience can't see the difference between characters, they'll be listening for

distinctive turns of phrase, accents, and speech patterns to help keep the characters straight.

- Scriptwriters should also choose precise words for script categories such as delivery directions and sound effects, even though listeners will never directly be aware of them. Is a character *laughing* as he or she speaks certain lines—or *giggling, chuckling,* or *guffawing* instead? Is another character *crying*—or *weeping, wailing, sniffling,* or getting "*choked up*"? You may also want to encourage groups of students to brainstorm precisely described sounds for sound effects (e.g., *thudding, hissing, humming, clanking*) to create a communal list from which they can draw as needed.

SKILLS FOCUS: MOOD

One of audio's strengths is how quickly it can create a mood and establish an atmosphere. Use the following suggestions to help students make the most of the possibilities in this respect:

- Leverage the power of music. What moods do certain genres or instruments evoke? Are violins and cellos naturally sad or romantic? Does electronic or dance music always lend an upbeat feeling to a scene? Why? Discuss these issues as a group. For students new to the impact of music, play passages from movie soundtracks. Ask them to guess what is happening, generally, in that particular scene in the movie. Those who are familiar with the movie can tell them how accurate they are.
- Create a wall chart of modifiers that can be used to describe music or delivery directions to set a particular mood. These might include *ominous, celebratory, lonely, boisterous, romantic, wacky, frightening, chaotic,* and *wistful.*
- Audio can be an oddly personal, even intimate, medium. Encourage students to include moments in their scripts where a character, news reporter, or host privileges the audience by sharing personal feelings and thoughts. Explain that doing this can help establish what might be called a psychological mood—that is, a sense of atmosphere created not through external sounds depicting "reality" but by people confiding their internal reaction to events: "The stadium and all the cheering fans started to swim before my eyes . . . and then I realized I was crying."
- Although dialogue can underscore the prevailing mood, students should know that they can actually heighten atmosphere by contrasting it with the characters' personal mood. For example, a script passage with characters being loud and carefree in a graveyard at midnight can call attention to how quiet, desolate, and somber the setting actually is.

SKILLS FOCUS: SPEAKING AND LISTENING

Students should write audio scripts with the idea that everything that they do should facilitate speaking, listening, or both. You can make the connection between composition and speaking/listening even stronger by introducing a few basic concepts. For example, audio scripts can use delivery directions and other techniques to be more expressive and effective. Here are three such areas to focus on:

1. *Volume/intensity.* Make this distinction for students by reading a line of text in a regular whisper and then a heated whisper. Invite them to suggest ways that both volume and intensity can be used for emphasis.
2. *Isolating a word or phrase.* Another method for adding emphasis, isolation can be indicated in scripts with an ellipsis or by setting off words with dashes.
3. *Repetition.* A well-chosen word might seem to obviate the need for repetition, but a strong word repeated as part of escalating emotion can be effective as well. As students revise their scripts, prompt them to ask themselves if any repetition is intentional or merely accidental.

Help students understand that it's not enough to employ these techniques in a wholesale manner, but they must do so strategically. After all, a radio play that doesn't sound natural because it's full of highly theatrical line readings is not likely to be successful. More important, the power of these techniques is diluted if they're used too frequently.

Here are some additional teachable points regarding speaking and listening:

- Insert pauses in scripts, especially in dialogue. Although "**dead air**" is frowned upon, the occasional moment of brief silence gives the audience a chance to reflect on what has happened or to anticipate what will.
- Using a microphone is a fairly straightforward and intuitive skill for most students. Still, you'll want to stress some basic rules that benefit both speakers and listeners. These include sitting close, but not too close, to the mic, and not touching its recording surface.
- During production, all eyes should be on the director, who will usually cue actors and other speakers with hand gestures of some sort.
- Tempo is key: Speaking at a brisk pace creates excitement, but the words must still be intelligible for listeners.
- Caution students about putting on an overly formal, contrived-sounding "radio announcer" voice, especially during news spots and PSAs. Instead, they should speak as if they're sharing some important

information with a small group made up of both friends and adults. Their tone should be conversational, but clear and using *language*–not a tone–that sounds slightly formal.

- In PSAs, news spots, and other expository or persuasive scripts, students should avoid having an anchor, announcer, or reporter quote somebody else directly. Instead, they should paraphrase that person: Attempting a direct quote too often results in awkward mimicry.
- Encourage students to practice many times and coach them not to expect to get it right the first time. Practicing reading scripts–that is, rehearsing them–provides the kind of repetition that is also great for building fluency, which is especially important for English Language Learners (Taguchi, Takayasu-Maass, & Gorsuch, 2004).

To maximize speaking and listening benefits, spend extra time reviewing with students what they may already know about writing effective dialogue. Remind them that since characters in radio dramas can't be shown and an external narrator must be used sparingly, dialogue must convey the lion's share of the action.

Also, point out that humorous dialogue can function effectively as comic relief, but to do so it must work in the context of a dramatic scene or relevant information (in nonfiction broadcasts, such as radio programs one might hear on NPR). It can't strike the listener as a stand-alone joke that was simply shoehorned into the script to get laughs.

Finally, explain that dialogue in drama and spoken text in other audio scripts should be energetic and connective–it keeps things moving and listeners listening. Students should avoid extended monologues, a monotone delivery style, and straight readings of passages that were originally intended solely as print texts.

LITERACY ACROSS THE DISCIPLINES: TIME-TRAVEL DIALOGUES

Encourage students to script monologues by famous figures from history, making sure that the text is informed by research and/or the content-area reading they're already doing in other disciplines. Provide as needed script and video samples of one-person shows based upon people such as Golda Meir, Franklin Delano Roosevelt, Mark Twain, and so on. Once students have developed a deep sense of how these people lived, what they believed, and how they spoke, challenge students to collaborate on a "Meeting of Minds"–style dialogue.

What would Thomas Jefferson say to Abraham Lincoln if the two met? Or what might Einstein have learned from Sally Ride if they had ever had a chance to hold a conversation?

THE WRITING PROCESS

Ideas for Prewriting

Prewriting often involves outlining the flow and structure of text. With this in mind, encourage students to craft radio scripts in which scenes shift rapidly, whether they are writing a news podcast or a drama. A brisk pace seems to be more vital to success in audio than in other media.

Have students write outlines for any multisegment podcasts. Some segments may not be scripted at all, such as roundtable discussions, spontaneous follow-up questions in interviews, or musical performances, but an overall outline will help writers plan for the flow between these and scripted segments.

Continue to emphasize audience and purpose. This is true for radio dramas in specific genres but also for news spots. For example, ask students if they'll be reporting on an event for informational reasons or to support some editorial or persuasive message as in a PSA.

Encourage students to be inventive when plotting the structure of their radio dramas. Point out that radio seems to excel in presenting flashbacks and flash-forwards. Explore this idea through discussion, helping students understand that since all the imagery takes place in the audience's mind, stories can jump around more easily in time and space. That said, scriptwriters should be mindful of clearly signaling the necessary transitions for listeners. Often these are most effectively accomplished through a combination of explicit dialogue or voice-over narration (e.g., "It was a bitterly cold winter's day four years ago when I first met her . . .") and matching sound effects or other devices that show a contrast with the present (e.g., sleigh bells jingling or dialogue now spoken through "chattering teeth.")

Ideas for Drafting

Consider creating a "verbal thesaurus" as a group; this would be a list of words that are easier to speak aloud than their synonyms (which, conversely, might work better in print). For example, *teacher*, with its strong initial consonant and simple, two-syllable pronunciation is a better "audio word" than *educator*. Students can refer to this thesaurus as they draft—and add new words to it as they draft, too.

Provide this tip to students: Have characters or on-air speakers ask questions that are left hanging. Listeners will stay tuned in to find out the answers, which are sometimes provided after a short **break** of some sort or sometimes much later in a broadcast or podcast (in cases where the questions are asked in an opening intro).

For the intro to a news broadcast or podcast, students should consider featuring a "**pull quote**" (an engaging, often thought-provoking, description or opinion) from a later part of the script. This can grab the attention of the audience, who will keep listening to learn more about the content previewed by this "**teaser**."

Remind students that they should add some kind of closing or wrap-up to the end of their script. This is an opportunity to remind listeners of upcoming episodes and thank anyone who helped make the broadcast possible.

Differentiated Instruction

Below-Level Students Can . . .

- Rehearse their scripts even as they're still drafting them. That is, they may find it helpful to read sections aloud in order to correct formatting and improve word choice on the fly.
- Use the techniques of recorded poetry—but not necessarily with poetry. Instead, they can write audio scripts based upon a reading or performance of *any* text that fits their ability level and their listeners' interests.
- Benefit from adjusting the amount of scriptwriting by including more room for spontaneity and ad-libbing according to their areas of strengths and weaknesses. For example, if students are more comfortable with oral than written language, their scripts can be kept leaner by supplementing them with index cards full of "talking points" or other forms of prompts or reminders.
- Gain confidence from the fact that audio is often more forgiving than other media: If something in the script doesn't quite work during execution, it's relatively easy to fix because speaking a revised version of a line is much less involved than, say, shooting a scene differently or redrawing a comics page.

Advanced Students Can . . .

- Act as "producers" and hosts for podcasts that encompass segments by multiple students. In this role, advanced students can script key transitions as well as the intro and wrap-up.
- Indulge in wordplay and other opportunities to exploit their vocabulary knowledge in a way that's entertaining for listeners. Point out that verbal wit is a key ingredient in audio.
- Write audio scripts with a cross-curricular slant, using their knowledge of audio scripts to bring to life a current event from social studies or science.

English Language Learners Can . . .

- Prepare for writing by listening to radio shows or podcasts in their native language in order to grasp the structural aspects of such shows and the formal elements of the medium (music, sound effects, and so on).
- Focus on the speaking and listening tips (see Skills Focus: Speaking and Listening, this chapter) on in order to improve their oral language skills.

- Make recordings of themselves reading, or acting out, sections of their scripts as part of the writing process. The act of listening to themselves encourages fluency because they will be motivated to fine-tune their scripts and rehearse their lines so that they can be "perfect" when it comes to the final recording or broadcast. This repeated reading of their own work will improve fluency (Rasinski, 1990) in a way that's far more engaging than, say, rereading passages from a leveled reader aloud.
- Write and record scripts in their primary language for their parents or other speakers of that language. Although this practice has its own value, it can also be used as a step toward translating the production into English and supporting English language development.
- Share recordings in other languages or from other countries so that their classmates can hear different styles and techniques. In English, they can introduce these recordings, noting audience and purpose, identifying well-known performers or news readers, and so on. (This might actually help all students because listening to audio texts in a language one *doesn't* understand can heighten appreciation for all the *non-spoken* elements that are present.)
- Use the scripting of sound effects to practice phonics skills in a way that doesn't seem "too young": by transcribing precise sounds they want to convey they will need to figure out their phonetic spellings.

Ideas for Revising

During the revision stage, students should reexamine each word choice they have made. Are the most vivid and precise forms of nouns and verbs used? Is figurative language used where it could be?

To help students identify areas for improvement, consider having them read the script aloud to someone who has not read any portion of it. They can then ask this "model listener" to identify which details are helpful and which parts of the script would benefit from using words that are less generic.

Encourage students to question themselves as to whether they have made use of the medium's unique aspects in the service of their audience and purpose. For example, are there any moments that they can present with greater impact by having a character or the host take on a confidential tone and speak to the listener as if they were alone?

Similarly, point out that their scripts may very well be clear, efficient, and informative. Yet does that mean that they have effectively evoked sensory imagery through word choice and auditory details?

Reproduce and distribute the Audio Revision Checklist in Appendix B. Advise students to refer to these as they strengthen their scripts through revision. Then you can use the Spoken Word and Audio Scripts rubric in Appendix C to evaluate their finished products.

WRAP-UP

You will probably find that, once they have learned these skills, students will pay greater attention to the nuances of language in all their writing. Although audio scripts do rely on music, sound effects, and other nonverbal elements, this chapter's focus on the primacy of the spoken word should enhance appreciation of, and motivation for learning, a range of related skills, benefits, and concepts. These might include the following:

1. An understanding of how syntax and sentence structure affect rhythm in spoken and written language and the ways that writers can achieve "musicality" generally in their work.
2. Critical listening skills regarding radio (or streaming audio) commercials and news reports: Each scripted word has been chosen for its impact, its denotation, and its precise meaning.
3. Increased confidence when it comes to public speaking–when students train themselves to read from preexisting scripts, it can eliminate some of the anxiety attached to the act of speaking to an audience.
4. Strategies for connecting ELA skills such as composition, speaking, and listening to technology curriculum such as podcasting–this is one of the easier ways that students can feel that they are creating "professional"-level media products (e.g., individuals and groups can make their podcasts available on the iTunes platform).

CHAPTER 3

COMICS AND GRAPHIC NOVEL SCRIPTS

Comics are fun to read, write, and draw, and they require comparatively little technical know-how or setup for even students who are quite young to start creating. However, to make comics (which include graphic novels and nonfiction) that leverage the full artistic or informational potential of the medium is a different matter, one that the study of scripts can make clear. Their format reflects the medium's equal attention to both text and imagery, and can be as intuitive to grasp as comics themselves, for a kind of "scaffolding" is built in as words and pictures naturally support each other. In addition, as writing products, scripts for comics and graphic novels represent logical stepping-stones for students who may be progressing from dramatic plays and audio scripts to scriptwriting for moving-image media such as movies.

WHY TEACH THIS?

Comics help visual learners master the basics of fiction and nonfiction narrative modes while providing ample opportunities to write description and exposition and to practice skills related to transitions, sequence/structure, and other areas. Assigning the creation of comic scripts can also be a great way to motivate student writing in response to literature, enrich content-area reading and writing (Jaffe & Monnin, 2012), and bolster the development of multiple literacies (Jacobs, 2007).

Common Core State Standards for Skills Focus

W.7.3. Write narratives to develop real or imagined experiences or events using effective technique, relevant descriptive details, and well-structured event sequences.

W.7.5. With some guidance and support from peers and adults, develop and strengthen writing as needed by planning, revising, editing, rewriting, or trying a new approach, focusing on how well purpose and audience have been addressed.

W.11–12.3. Write narratives to develop real or imagined experiences or events using effective technique, well-chosen details, and well-structured event sequences.

W.11–12.3c. Use a variety of techniques to sequence events so that they build on one another to create a coherent whole and build toward a particular tone and outcome (e.g., a sense of mystery, suspense, growth, or resolution).

W.11–12.5. Develop and strengthen writing as needed by planning, revising, editing, rewriting, or trying a new approach, focusing on addressing what is most significant for a specific purpose and audience. (NGA Center & CCSSO, 2010, pp. 42–46)

Skills Preview

In this chapter, you'll learn to help students do the following:

- Plan the structure of narratives by using a graphic organizer specifically geared to comics
- Improve their editing skills by having them work authentically as peer editors
- Analyze and choose the best strategies for developing characters in fiction
- Practice a variety of visual literacy skills that can be applied to reading and writing across a range of media

GETTING STARTED

Pictures, pictures, pictures—that's what people see when they flip through the pages of a graphic novel or a comic book. Yes, there's text, too, often a lot of it, but the tendency is to think of comics as a "visual medium."

Because of the emphasis on graphics, then, it's not surprising that some students may not know that most comics actually start with a script. Even those creators who are "cartoonists"—meaning that they both write and draw a comic—often work with some form of script to develop story structure and plan dialogue. (To demonstrate this point vividly, and the overarching principle of why prewriting is so crucial to graphic storytelling, consider using the QuickStart Follow-up activity.)

Oh, and a quick note on terminology: Please know that *comics* is the umbrella term I'll be using for this medium (McCloud, 1993)—comic strips, comic books, graphic novels, graphic nonfiction, and manga are all subcategories that share the same basic storytelling approach and script format.

QuickStart: Gag Cartoons and "Backward" Scripting

The heart of scripting comics can be conveyed by taking a look at the medium in its most pared-down format: the single-**panel** cartoon like the kind found on newspaper editorial pages or in The *New Yorker*. Have students share what they know about such works, perhaps reviewing what they may have learned about political cartoons in social studies or history classes (see this chapter's Literacy Across the Disciplines). If you can provide an example or two, great. But be aware that some students may be able to quickly sketch one from memory on the chalkboard.

Point out that such humorous "gag cartoons" usually contain a **caption**, but they also can feature text (such as labels and signs) in the art itself and sometimes **word balloons** as well. The key idea here is that it's the combination of text *plus* art that constitutes the comics medium, regardless of scale.

Divide the class into two groups. One group should brainstorm for sentence starters in the imperative mood that sound formal and "official" (such as "Please utilize all due caution . . . ," "Refrain from unruly behavior while . . . ," and so on). The second group should brainstorm for humorous anthropomorphic images and characters—a talking banana or pickle, or a "funny animal" with human traits—and sketch them on the board or a display easel.

Then make the two sets of information available to both groups, and have students spend a few minutes scripting a gag cartoon, using the following simple format and the humor inherent in the contrast of the serious and the absurd. Explain that this activity reflects the creative process used in any type of comics boiled down to its simplest elements.

Description of Art: _____

Caption: _____

Have groups share these mini-scripts by reading them aloud. Choose one or more to "produce" by simply drawing the art and lettering the caption beneath it. Then have students reflect on how the process and results might be different if they were free to make up both the visuals and the text. Explain that this is the essence of what scriptwriters do in the field of comics and graphic novels.

QuickStart Follow-up: Running out of Real Estate

Once you've finished creating a single-panel cartoon as a group and have drawn a border around it, add word balloons and invite students to provide humorous dialogue—but do not limit them or tell them to stop; instead, keep adding their text and erasing bits of the artwork to accommodate the space it requires within the border. If students suggest adding a second panel, you can do so, but instruct a student artist to sketch generously within its panel border, and then quickly fill that one with text as you did the first one, erasing the art as you do so. Guide students to grasp that the finite space available on any single page or in any single panel creates a "zero-sum" situation in which the amount of text automatically delimits the amount of art, and vice versa. In order to avoid rework and losing either text or art, the coordination of these two elements must be worked out to some degree in advance. That's where the value of a script comes in.

An Even Quicker Start . . .

On the last page of each issue, *The New Yorker* usually runs a captionless cartoon as part of a contest for readers to devise a caption for it. Choose one or two of these for your students and ask them to provide captions for them verbally as a whole-group activity. Alternatively, you could choose any visually humorous gag cartoon or political cartoon, remove the caption, and share it with students to elicit possible captions. In either scenario, draw attention to the way that the humor derives from the combination of both art *and* words.

Learn the Lingo

bird's-eye view: An extreme overhead point of view. Art rendered from this perspective is good for providing a literal "overview" of the action or setting in a way that shows where things are in relation to each other.

breakdowns/thumbnails: Rough sketches, often created by an artist and writer together, that show how the action and plot points in a comics story will "break down" on a page-by-page and panel-by-panel basis. Breakdowns help answer creative questions such as "How many panels should we use for that important conversation?" and "How large should the panels be in the big battle scene?" *Thumbnails* simply refers to the same type of sketch but at a much smaller scale. They feature rougher images, and they are small enough for several pages of comics art to fit on a single sheet of paper.

caption aka narrative/caption box: The rectangular boxes that appear along the top or bottom edges of a panel. The text in them can represent the author's voice providing narration ("Our story begins in a quiet town . . ."), simple transitions ("Meanwhile, in a warehouse across town . . ."), or more-involved information, especially in graphic nonfiction.

double-page splash: A large single piece of artwork that occupies both a left-hand page and a right-hand page facing each other, often used for confrontations or to present a wide, spectacular vista. Scriptwriters should keep the ultimate method of publishing in mind: There will only be spreads such as this when the comic is constructed as a booklet. If individual one-sided sheets are stapled together, there will be no spreads—although there will be twice as many **page-flips**.

over-the-shoulder shot: Shot composed as if standing right behind someone, usually a speaker in a conversation or interview.

page-flip: The key device used in creating narrative breaks in comics story structure. When readers turn a page, the entire scene can be shifted to a new setting with different characters and, because the turning itself signals a shift, supplying transitional text is not as important.

panel: The basic storytelling unit of comics; sometimes incorrectly called a "frame," a panel is much more than geometric border around content and sometimes doesn't even have clearly marked borders. Remind students that the leap from one panel to the next can span seconds or centuries, inches or miles–it all depends on the print and visual information that the script gives to readers.

semi-splash: A half-page splash used to underscore dramatic moments. A semi-splash is often used at the end of a chapter or issue to heighten the impact of a cliffhanger. (See also *splash page* below.)

sound effects/SFX: In comics, the arrangement of oversized block letters to denote a sound (e.g., "CRASH!" for a crashing sound). These can also be used for laughter ("Ha ha ha"), songs and music, and really anything else writers want readers to "hear" apart from spoken dialogue. A comic book letterer typically handles these.

splash page: A comics page consisting entirely of a single panel. As the name would imply, this page is intended to "make a splash." It is usually the first page in a typical comic book and features a striking, dramatic image that pulls readers into the story. It is used less often in graphic novels.

spread break: The break between the bottom of a left-hand page and the top of the opposite right-hand page. Comics writers often use this natural pause in reading to start a new scene or shift the setting without using a caption to alert readers.

thought bubble: A text field that conveys a character's private thoughts, usually with a trail of bubbles in diminishing size leading back to the character's head. Iconic images such as dark clouds and Valentine's Day–style hearts can be inserted into a thought bubble to express emotions graphically.

word balloon (aka "speech balloon"): A balloon-shaped text field in a comic in which dialogue appears. Most students will already be familiar with the fact that dialogue belongs in balloons with a "tail" that points to the speaker's mouth. What they might not realize is that a speaker can have multiple small balloons in a single panel, especially if the dialogue is exchanged with another character.

worm's-eye view: An image with a perspective taken at ground level. This technique is typically used for dramatic effect to make characters or settings seem "bigger than life."

COMICS SCRIPT TYPES

Review as necessary what students already know about the format of *any* type of script. Point out that scripts for traditional "floppy" comic books, newspaper-style comic strips, or graphic novels similarly contain the following:

- Descriptions of settings
- Dialogue and suggestions for how characters speak it
- "Stage" directions

Make the Connection: Using "Shots"

This chapter concerns itself with the "full-script" method of making comics, a style that resembles a movie script: All the dialogue is present even in the earliest draft, the visuals are specified in detail, and the art team's job is to "realize" the script just as a film crew brings a screenplay to life. (Another, more collaborative process, involves a "rough script," called that because the artist has more input and dialogue is not finalized until art is drawn.) However, unlike with a screenplay (see Chapter 4 on "overdirecting"), the comics writer who crafts a full script pretty much calls the shots.

And that word—*shots*—turns out to be a key one.

That's because anyone writing comics would do well to learn some of the basic terminology used in film and TV scripts. So don't hesitate to share the "Learn the Lingo" terms from Chapter 4 at this time, since many comics scripts employ the same terminology as is used by screenwriters. Even if your students won't write movies anytime soon, being familiar with concepts such as close-ups and establishing shots can only help them when scripting graphic narratives.

Graphic novels, so popular in recent years, are merely book-length works of fiction in comics form that can come in the same genres as prose fiction. Similarly, graphic nonfiction can appear in the subgenres of graphic history, graphic memoir, graphic how-to, and so on. The basic relationship between word and image–that they reinforce, elaborate, or clarify each other in a variety of ways–holds true regardless; only the strategies that writers or cartoonists employ change in response to shifts in genre, audience, purpose, and so on. For example, a didactic how-to comic might feature many more close-ups so details can be easily apprehended by readers, and more flamboyant uses of lettering may be avoided in favor of a more conservative approach wherein easy-to-read labels are prized.

With this underlying commonality in mind–the content of scripts may vary widely but there are not different *types* of them per se–this chapter will move fluidly between comic strips, comic books, and lengthier forms such as graphic novels without focusing separately on each. Clearly this is unlike Chapter 2, where scripts for recorded poetry, radio drama, and newscasts were shown to be quite different.

Manga

Japanese comics, or manga, are very popular with young people these days, so some of your students may ask whether they can try their hand at writing in this style. The answer is yes, they can script a variety of genres for manga, including fantasy, action, and sports stories, and generally they should follow the same guidelines and processes as other scripts.

There is one major difference, however: Traditional manga reads right to left at the page-, panel-, and within-panel levels. Therefore, all manga scripts would start with describing what's on the *last* page—not the conclusion of the story, but what would be the last page if you held a book with the binding on the right, as opposed to the left, as in the West.

Confused yet? Well, you probably needn't worry since any students who want to script manga can explain the layout and page navigation, perhaps even by using a volume from their own collection as a prop. In terms of format, there are no major differences. Manga scripts tend to pay more attention to the size of sound effects (distinguishing between small, medium, and large), and diehard fans-turned-writers may want to incorporate a handful of Japanese terms, but really the only critical thing to bear in mind when reading or writing them is that on any given comics page "panel 1" would appear in the upper right corner, not the upper left.

Graphic Novels and Graphic Nonfiction

Some of your students may aspire to scripting full-length graphic novels. If your curriculum allows for a project of such scope, remind students that the basic elements of comics scriptwriting still apply. More likely your curriculum pace will not allow for this investment of time. However, you can encourage students to continue on their own, and perhaps find a time later in the semester or year when you can allow students to share completed projects. If students do, in fact, take on this endeavor, celebrate this learning! You have truly succeeded if students want to continue class work on their own time.

In any case, make sure that these ambitious scriptwriters keep these additional points in mind:

- A book map (see Skills Focus: Story Structure, this chapter) becomes even more important when planning a work in excess of ten pages (fewer than that is mini-comic territory) or 10–30 pages (the length of a typical comics story or comic book).
- Who will draw and letter such a long work? Even if writers do it themselves, the time difference between scripting and producing comics becomes magnified over the length of an entire book. Are students prepared to wait that long to see the finished result?
- As stated above, focus on one part of the graphic novel—a chapter or a group of short chapters or sections. The rest of the graphic novel can then be developed later from this core beginning.
- Think about collaborating. Different teams can script and then produce separate chapters that, when compiled, form a graphic novel. Roles such as story editor, art editor, and production editor can be assigned to ensure visual and narrative continuity as well as keeping the teams on schedule and trafficking the different pieces.
- A graphic novel and a collection of comic books are two different things. Often the latter are gathered in a trade paperback format, but

these are not true graphic novels as they are not self-contained works of fiction in the manner of prose novels, but rather narrative excerpts from series that may have started many years before the story in hand and continued long after. So students who wish to collect a substantial series of comic strips, mini-comics, or comic books can still do so as a form of publishing their work.

- Have your students consider writing a graphic memoir instead, a popular subgenre of graphic nonfiction. That way, writers can draw upon incidents and details from their own lives, thus concentrating on storytelling rather than on building a fictional world from scratch.
- The drawn images in graphic nonfiction should, whenever possible, be based upon "photo reference." The scriptwriter can attach these to the script itself, perhaps even using personal photos if the topic or setting is local, or if the script is for a graphic memoir. If the script is for a graphic history, then archival images must be researched in the same way as digital stories are (see Chapter 5), with the obvious exception that the photos themselves would not be used, so there are no issues to be resolved regarding copyright or permission.

MAKING FRIENDS WITH THE FORMAT

Reproduce for your students the following professional script model of a graphic memoir/history, explaining that the precise format is not as universal as those used in, say, radio or film. For example, some comics scripts may have each chunk of dialogue numbered so that the letterer knows the order in which characters should speak. That's not the case with *March: Book One*, John L. Lewis's graphic story of his life during the civil rights movement. In the section reproduced here, the year is 1960 and, in response to racist violence, students at Tennessee State University have marched on Nashville City Hall to demand an end to segregation.

Lewis was assisted in this creative project by co-writer Andrew Aydin and award-winning artist Nate Powell, and, as you'll see from Powell's notes, the collaborative process was quite open: The script was followed, but the artist also expanded on its content, turning one page of script into two pages of finished story and art. That's not uncommon, but typically an editor will approve such changes to make sure that the length and structure of the overall text remains workable.

As a way of immersing themselves in the conventions of the medium (and the script format), consider having volunteers first make quick sketches of what this comics page (or two comics pages, per Powell's comments about the added content) might look like. Then you can reveal the finished book pages to spur analysis and reflection. How were student interpretations of the script different from Powell's, whose art and lettering can be seen following the model script?

p. 75 [pages 116–117 in final book]

Panel 1: C. T. VIVIAN and MAYOR WEST, wearing a bow tie and hat, trade polite but firm barbs.

> C. T. VIVIAN
> We are outraged at this bombing! How can you allow this sort of behavior in Nashville?! It's a miracle no one was killed!

> MAYOR WEST
> Mr. Vivian, let me say—

> C. T. VIVIAN
> No, I'll say. This has gone too far.

Panel 2: Close-up on MAYOR WEST.

> MAYOR WEST
> You all have the power to destroy this city, so let's not have any mobs. I will do everything I can to enforce the laws without prejudice, but I have no power to force restaurant owners to serve people they do not want to.

Panel 3: From over the shoulder of MAYOR WEST, looking out onto C. T. VIVIAN, DIANE NASH, JOHN LEWIS, and the gathered masses. A student from the line speaks out.

> MAYOR WEST
> We are all Christians together—so let us pray together.

> STUDENT
> How about *eating* together?!

Panel 4: DIANE NASH steps forward clutching a typed list of questions.

Artist's Comment: *A seven-panel page can get pretty crowded, and Mayor West is making an important decision here. It's crucial to have enough time/space in the pages to provide for pauses revealing the tension, consideration, and doubt in this scene, so I expanded the script into two comic pages.*

Comics scripts can be flexible and need not always follow this format: Dialogue can be set flush left, with colons after the speakers' names. The key information for the artist and letterer is the panel number and the order of spoken text.

Note the use of a specific kind of shot here. Scriptwriters often do this in order to accentuate the drama of a given moment.

Artist's Comment: *I added some casual transitional dialogue ("Look—") here to keep the exchange believable. Few people are as concise as may be presented in script dialogue, and little interjections are great tools to maintain a rhythm with the panels and text.*

An **over-the-shoulder** ("OTS") shot is common not only in comics, but in film, TV, and video.

Here is another place where the artist added a panel, as you'll see when looking at the fifth panel in the finished pages. Also added was an off-panel voice, prompting the mayor. Off-panel dialogue must be used when the artwork is a close-up on a different character.

March: Book One © 2013 John Lewis and Andrew Aydin

                              DIANE NASH
                    Will you use the prestige of your
                    office to appeal to the citizens to
                    stop racial discrimination?

                              MAYOR WEST
                    I appeal to all citizens to end
                    discrimination, to have no bigotry,
                    no bias, no hatred.

Panel 5:

                              DIANE NASH
                    Do you mean that to include lunch
                    counters?

                              MAYOR WEST
                    Little lady, I stopped segregation
                    seven years ago at the airport when
                    I first took office, and there has
                    been no trouble there since.

                              DIANE NASH
                    Then, Mayor, do you recommend that
                    the lunch counters be desegregated?

Panel 6: Close-up, MAYOR WEST.

                              MAYOR WEST
                    Yes.

Panel 7: The crowd erupts into cheers and
applauds.

                              MAYOR WEST
                    [weakly]. . . that's up to the store
                    managers, of course.

Artist's Comment: *It's important to show Mayor West's silent reaction to Diane's comment, revealing his shame and cowardice within that second's pause. I inserted a panel that allows the reader to empathize with him as he realizes he's made a mistake. I also inserted text for Diane Nash to refocus the mayor.*

Artist's Comment: *The second page has slightly larger panels for the mayor's historic decision, and to provide a "beat" on which to end the scene. I removed the borders on this panel to suspend the passage of time, and altered the mayor's lettering to imply that his decree may not actually be followed at first.*

The [weakly] is like a delivery direction provided to an actor—although of course there is no actor involved.

March: Book One by John Lewis, Andrew Aydin, and Nate Powell (www.topshelfcomix.com)

March: Book One by John Lewis, Andrew Aydin, and Nate Powell (www.topshelfcomix.com)

SKILLS FOCUS: STORY STRUCTURE

Have you noticed how much of comics lingo relates to pages—how they are laid out and how they work together? Unlike in prose text, *where* something is presented in a comic—its precise location on a particular page—is critical. This is true not only because comic books usually have a set number of pages to work with, but also because creators need to use devices such as **splash pages** and page-flip transitions strategically and plan what the overall experience will be for the reader.

To this end, you may want to have students use a book map to plan their comics story (see Figure 3.1). First, though, you may want to review the structural elements of any successful story, such as grabbing the reader's attention, using conflict and obstacles to move the narrative forward, and organizing the drama according to rising and falling action. Even if students' stories will be as brief as four pages, a book map will help them determine the order and visual presentation of such key plot points and devices for readers.

Share the book map model in Figure 3.1, where each of the boxes corresponds to a page. Introduce it to students as a kind of visual outline or graphic organizer determining what the flow of the comic will be like for readers and helping scriptwriters ensure that they can fit everything. (Clarify that breakdowns, in contrast, are mostly used for detailed, page-level planning and thus are considerably larger.) Students can fill in the boxes with sketches or brief phrases that describe what will happen in their stories, or a combination of the two. If the scripts will be longer, this same book map pattern is simply repeated until the final page.

Figure 3.1. A Four-Page Book Map for a Mini-Comic

Note that a comic, like all Western-style books, always begins on a right-hand side. It is only after turning this page that readers encounter the first spread.

Instead of being a story page in a four-page comics story, page one could also be the cover for a two- or three-page story that would begin on the next left-hand page.

In this example, pages 2 and 3 form the only spread. In a longer story, spreads would appear on pages 4–5, 6–7, and so on.

The final left-hand page, which in this case is page 4, could also be a back cover. Then the story would have to conclude on page 3.

As students use their book maps to plan their narratives prior to scripting, you might want them to consider the following questions. These will help them focus on the dramatic structure and tempo of their story but in terms that are practical (and visual) rather than abstract.

- What are the most dramatic moments, and where do they occur?
- How much of your story is spent setting things up before the main plot kicks in?
- Are the climax and/or resolution too abrupt?
- Do you need more, or fewer, pages to tell your story effectively?
- How will including devices such as splash pages and **double-page splashes** affect the pacing and structure of your story? Will they, for example, force you to "rush" the ending by leaving you too little room?
- Are you using the page-flip to introduce surprises, plot reversals (e.g., a different character suddenly has the upper hand), or dramatic reveals of new information?

SKILLS FOCUS: CHARACTERIZATION

It might not be evident at first glance, but comics present an almost diagrammatic way of analyzing the process of character development: Dialogue and action are clearly separated.

This means that you can lead a guided reading of almost any worthy graphic novel and focus on how compelling characters are created—and then help students apply the same principles to their own scriptwriting. First, review with students what they already know about characterization, and have them slot relevant techniques or examples into one of these three approaches to conveying a character's personality to readers:

- *What the character says or does.* This includes how characters move or look. How do they dress? How do they furnish their homes? Do they have a signature phrase, movement, or skill?
- *What other characters say or do in relation to the character.* Do they treat the character a certain way? Do they say mean, or admiring, things about him or her?
- *What an author directly tells readers about the character.* Examples include any text in which we are given biographical background or information from an omniscient point of view (e.g., "Peter Parker was a noted bookworm at his high school").

A close reading of most comics pages will demonstrate how professional writers use these different approaches. You might want to share such a page with students and have them identify instances of each of the above techniques.

If possible, scan and display the page for the whole group, and invite students to mark each of these approaches with a different color to conduct a visual analysis of the strategies employed.

Very quickly they should begin to appreciate how effective writers use a balanced approach to create three-dimensional characters in a way that also helps vary the narrative presentation. Supplement your text-specific analysis with the following critical-thinking questions that build an appreciation of how scripts leverage the medium's formal features to develop characters:

- What would the effect be on readers if you only read what other characters said or thought about a character but never encountered a word balloon or a caption? (Sample answer: The character might seem distant to us as we are never given an "interior" view.)
- How would readers feel if a disproportionate amount of information were conveyed through a know-it-all narrator, with hardly any spoken dialogue or thought balloons? (Sample answer: Readers might feel that the character is not real to them but rather just an "idea.")
- What impression would you have of a character who has several lengthy **thought bubbles** on every page? (Sample answer: The character thinks too much, "living inside" his or head. Or a reader might feel that the story is slow, with not enough action.)

When it comes to writing their own scripts, students should therefore bear in mind that the way the character *appears*, the *information* provided in a caption, and the *text* in balloons and bubbles all work together to create compelling characters to which readers feel connected.

In addition, there are three optional tools that you can use to enrich the process of teaching characterization with comics. Even students who might not typically be engaged by the process of developing characters will probably be motivated by one of the following:

- *Series "bible".* This is an updatable document of no set length that anchors the creative decisions that are made in a comics series or even a comics "universe." It's where all new writers or artists turn to learn the history of the characters and their adventures and to maintain continuity with stories that already exist. You can motivate reluctant prose writers through this combination of expository writing (it's informational in nature) and creative writing (the information is largely made up) by assigning it as a precursor to scripting. Or consider having students loosely collaborate in small groups by having them share some of the same cast of characters. Then they can work together to draft a common bible, perhaps with each member taking on a separate aspect of their shared fictional world (biographies, settings, and so on).

- *Character designs.* Comics writers often spend considerable time conceptualizing the physical appearance of their characters. Is the character tall or short? Angular or soft-featured? In terms of attire, what does he or she wear that reflects a personal style, and if this is a superhero we're talking about, what does the costume look like? What are its colors and materials? Explain that the goal of illustrated character designs is to create a common reference for anyone who could possibly work with the characters, so writers need to explain to artists just what it is they're envisioning. Often character designs featuring different views of a character are incorporated into the series bible, which is primarily a text document but which can include key visuals as well.
- *Backstories.* Point out to students that even if the comic they create is the very first story to feature a given character, that character still has a "backstory" or prior history. You can encourage students to flesh this out by having them write an additional summary statement in the form of a biography or by filling out a character questionnaire that you develop as a group.

SKILLS FOCUS: PEER EDITING

Students may tend to think of editing as the revision of their own work—and rightly so. However, creating comics scripts provides an authentic way to practice editing skills that students can later transfer to their revision processes more broadly because in comics, editors and writers work very closely together. Therefore, you may want to replicate this dynamic by partnering writers and editors from the beginning.

That means that before writers script even a word, they can share their ideas and prewriting materials in a "story conference" with their editors. For their part, editors can ask questions concerning how writers plan to do the following:

- Develop their characters (see the related Skills Focus, this chapter)
- Structure their narratives dramatically (see the related Skills Focus, this chapter)
- Meet the expectations of their audience in terms of genre and style
- Leverage the unique elements of comics (e.g., captions, written sound effects, thought bubbles)

Later, during the revision stage, peer editors can keep the following checklist in mind as they read and review scripts, supplementing it with the self-editing tool, the Comics and Graphic Novel Revision Checklist (Appendix B), as needed:

- Are there briefer ways to say this?
- Will everything fit on the page as it's currently scripted?
- Is there a fluid connection between the panels, or is there too much of a story jump between them?
- In contrast, does the script *not* allow readers to make jumps they *can* handle, forcing the story to move more slowly than it needs to?
- Does the writing leverage the different elements that are unique to comics, using thought balloons and captions as well as word balloons?
- Does the structure make sense? Is there such an emphasis on scenes of action, for example, that the overall context for, and meaning of, that action can't be appreciated? Are there places where the writer can use text features such as cross-section diagrams, maps, or handwritten notes from a character to be make the writing clear or engaging?

LITERACY ACROSS THE DISCIPLINES: CARTOONING IN POLITICS AND SCIENCE

Much of this chapter has dealt with issues that largely concern fiction, such as dramatic structure and characterization. However, because of the clarity with which they illustrate difficult or abstract concepts, comics are a great medium for nonfiction.

With this in mind, consider practicing literacy skills in social studies by building upon this chapter's QuickStart activities. Just ask students to share single-panel political cartoons from editorial pages and discuss how these function as succinct, visual editorials. Students can be asked to script a cartoon that comments on a current or historical issue, political group, or leader. You might point out that political cartoons require both artistic creativity *and* a decision about the political perspective of the cartoon.

For science, students can be asked to script single-panel cartoons or three-panel comic strips that illustrate a process or a law in biological, chemical, environmental, or physical science. These can be played straight or incorporate humor. For example, a cartoon about cell division could be straightforward or make a joke about separation anxiety.

In both content areas the scripts should reflect the critically important use of labels, which can be designated like this:

LABEL1 [on dog]: Labor
LABEL2 [on bone]: Reduced Work Week
LABEL3 [on master's hand]: Management

One important distinction between the disciplines that both scriptwriters and artists should keep in mind is that while caricature and exaggeration are acceptable in political cartoons, scientifically oriented art must generally be more accurate if it is to be used for informational as well as entertainment purposes.

If students choose to write expository scripts about topics in science or social studies, have them consider using the device of a "guide" character who can speak conversationally to the reader. For example, in a comic about history, a time-traveling narrator might be a good way to present material. Similarly, a guide who can shrink to a subatomic size can more easily teach readers about electrons. Again, scripting comics allows students to approach nonfiction content-area writing by using creative techniques that probably wouldn't work (and might even seem bizarre) in prose compositions.

THE WRITING PROCESS

Ideas for Prewriting

If students choose a nonfiction topic, make sure they research it and gather information using reliable sources just as they would when writing prose. If students choose to write fiction, allow them to create and use tools, such as a book map, character designs, and a "bible," as needed.

For students writing fiction, remind them that, as with radio drama, comic book scripts allow them to explore genres (science fiction, historical fiction) that might be too hard to address in a movie or video script. For those writing nonfiction, encourage them to think about the visual nature of the medium and how they might capitalize on it by including text features, such as maps, charts, and cross-sections.

As a time-saver, consider having students adapt an assignment they have already written into comics form. Coach them to add, omit, or change material as necessary to fit the new medium instead of simply "pouring" content into it.

Do some of your students, perhaps having already had some experience creating comics, want to try writing a full-length graphic novel? That's fine, but have them choose a single incident, scene, or chapter to work on first (see the \ Graphic Novels section, this chapter). Point out that many graphic novels were serialized first as comic books much like Dickens' novels were serialized. Students can plan a longer story, but the segment of it that they actually write now should stand on its own and be dramatically satisfying.

All students will benefit from using some form of visual organizer. Remind them that they can map out the flow of the story page-by-page using a book map, and/or break down the panel-by-panel storytelling by quickly sketching some **thumbnails** until they hit upon a structure that works. Breakdowns, sometimes called "page breakdowns" or "panel breakdowns," need not be done in thumbnail form, of course, but it makes sense to conceptualize the storytelling rapidly at the early stages instead of investing added effort into making larger and more detailed sketches before some sort of initial consensus is achieved.

Ideas for Drafting

Remind students that they are writing for two audiences and two purposes—to create an engaging or informative text for readers and also to provide clear, practical directions for artists and letterers.

Clarify your expectations in terms of punctuation and capitalization. Many comics use a font that features all caps. They can also feature exaggerated end punctuation, such as a row of exclamation points. Make sure students understand the ground rules and criteria by which you'll be evaluating their scripts in terms of conventional grammar, usage, and mechanics.

Encourage writers to script a caption that summarizes a series of actions or events that isn't essential for the reader to witness, or even to include a text-only panel as a transition to new panels that return to the inclusion of art.

Like writing for newspapers or composing certain forms of poetry, writing comics teaches the importance of concision. Unlike in journalism or poetry, however, there is no set limit on the number of words or lines in the text. Instead, students should bear in mind that every word they add to word balloons, thought bubbles, and captions has the potential to expand the size of each element and therefore reduce the available space for art. To help students approach this issue in a practical way, have them analyze a favorite comic or manga. How many words, on average, appear in each panel? This figure can serve as a guideline. How many words are in the most text-heavy panels? This can act as a word count "ceiling" for their own scripts.

Challenge students to contrast what's in a thought bubble with what's actually said by the same character in the same panel. Can this be a means of showing a character's anxiety? Or perhaps to illustrate a two-faced nature, by having the character say one thing while thinking another? Explain that comics provide a clear and efficient way to do things that in prose and other media might be too tricky or clunky.

Writers should tweak elements such as the descriptions of word balloon shapes for greater expressiveness. Does one in particular have an "electric" design with jagged points and a lightning-like tail to signify excitement, intensity, or rage? Or should another balloon be somewhat shapeless and blobby to convey sadness? Point out that it's fine for the script to include such information for the letterer to use—even if that letterer turns out to be the writer.

Students might not be aware of how much is left out of comics, and therefore the degree to which comics writers streamline stories by forcing readers to make inferences. For example, a shot of Spider-Man saying he's going home can immediately be followed by a panel depicting him swinging over rooftops: The storytelling omits showing details of how he opened a window, then shot a web to a nearby building, and so on. In this way, students can practice paring their narratives down to the essentials.

Onomatopoeia is a creative device that students often find few opportunities to use in their own writing. But in comics it's practically ubiquitous—in sound effects. Consider brainstorming sound effects with students and creating a class menu from which they can choose when drafting their scripts. These might include obvious examples such as "Bang!" but also more subtle ones such as "hissss." Regarding the latter, point out that alternate spellings are allowed in sound effects as long as readers can discern their meanings. For example, the sound of a slowly creaking door might be signaled in a script by "creeeeeak."

Differentiated Instruction

Advanced Students Can . . .

- Collaborate on a multipart work by planning an overarching plot, then scripting individual comics that then become different chapters; the end product need not be a full-blown graphic novel but perhaps an interconnected series of four- or six-page stories that can be read in sequence.
- Tell their stories through multiple, shifting points-of-view by calling for different styles of narrative captions in their scripts by spec'ing fonts or background fill colors that correspond to various characters.
- Experiment with different ways of using captions to add complexity and create more interesting narrative textures. For example, in addition to an omniscient narrator, some captions could be used to signify one of the characters telling the story; and if both types of captions are employed, the latter can be differentiated by having its text placed inside quotes so that readers attribute it to a character rather than to the author.
- Adapt narratives across media, using the story elements in a TV series or movie in their scripts. Encourage these students to think critically during the process— what aspects of their favorite show would be lost in the transition to comics? For example, how might their scripts make up for the role that music plays in shaping mood?
- Enjoy using the terminology for specific types of "shots" in their scripts (see the "Make the Connection" activity) that is part of moving-image media just as the professional model in this chapter used a close-up and an over-the-shoulder shot; other options include establishing shots, **reaction shots**, and overhead shots.

English Language Learners Can . . .

- Spend more time on the breakdowns than other students, adding more detail than is typical. They can then add another stage—working with you or other personal or reference resources—to label items and ideas that represent unfamiliar vocabulary. Then they will be ready to include these new words in their scripts.
- Narrate their breakdowns (or even finished art) verbally. Then, either you or a native English speaking student can coach them to find the precise words and phrases that help them convey the story they are trying to tell. ELLs can then include these in their finished script.
- Benefit from your paying extra attention to the lingo of comics, which may seem too specialized and esoteric. You can use gestures and sketches on a chalkboard to clarify terms such as *bubble*, *balloon*, and *splash* by showing students how the most common and therefore literal meanings of these words are instead used figuratively in comics scripts. For example, you might want to introduce the idiom "make a splash" and then ask students how it's related to the idea of a full-page image. You might even want to decorate a helium balloon with bits of dialogue on it, depending on the age of your students.

Below-Level Students Can . . .

- Write scripts that call for more silent panels. Remind them that wordless storytelling is perfectly acceptable in comics, but also that they will still need to describe the action sufficiently in the script so that dialogue and caption text is unnecessary.
- Spend time visualizing the content of each panel in detail before putting it into words. If students can first express the story action verbally, using their breakdowns as touchstones, then they may experience the writing process as less daunting because they must simply translate the "pictures" in their minds to the page.
- Adapt works that they have already written for your class or for another class, or a professional text that they have read, to help reinforce their comprehension of curricular content and make the writing process more accessible. That way they can repurpose everything from dialogue to facts that they have already researched and therefore focus on story structure, their script's descriptive passages, and so on.
- Pause and self-monitor during drafting to identify the sections of the script that are intended only for their collaborators versus those that readers will see.
- Create "original English language" manga instead of traditional manga if they are fans of that format; that way they can freely write scripts that call for manga-style art and typical manga character-types (i.e., no superheroes) but whose stories are told in conventional left-to-right manner.

Ideas for Revising

Introduce students, or invite them to introduce to one another, some of the basic items in a cartoonist's visual toolkit, such as "worry" lines, "motion" lines, and "impact" lines. These can be added to a script while revising to make descriptions of images more precise for the artist.

As with movie and television scripts, part of the scriptwriter's job is to provide enough, but not too much, visual fodder for collaborators—the collaborators need to be allowed to have creative input as well. Have students ask themselves whether they have been too restrictive when drafting. If so, they need not eliminate details but rather should rephrase some of them as suggestions or options.

Urge students to double-check their scripts to make sure that any assumptions they have about characters or setting actually make it to the page. Since virtually anything can be drawn, scripts need to be precise on important details, or artists may use a free hand to draw things that run counter to a writer's expectations. Ask students to think about questions such as these: *Does it matter how tall your main character is? Does it matter whether he or she is left- or right-handed? If so, you need to mention it.*

Although comics scripts are not intended to be read aloud, the revision stage may benefit from partners or small groups acting out certain passages or even the entire script if time permits. Writers should pay attention to, and take notes on, items such as the flow of the dialogue, the logic of the plot or sequence of ideas, and whether any of the "actors" has trouble reading or understanding the draft.

Revisit the three questions about building characters (Skills Focus: Characterization). Has the writer used a variety of visual and narrative strategies for characterization?

If they're using the peer editing techniques (see Skills Focus: Peer Editing), have writers check in with their editors to go over any major changes or simply confirm at key points that they're on the right track.

Reproduce and distribute the Comics and Graphic Novel Revision Checklist in Appendix B. Advise students to refer to these as they strengthen their scripts through revision. Also consider sharing the Comics and Graphic Novel Scripts rubric in Appendix C.

WRAP-UP

You will probably find that, once having become familiar with scripting graphic fiction and nonfiction, students will become much more strategic in all of their writing: They will increasingly value the placement of key ideas and information after working in this highly structured narrative framework with its clear and distinct "chunks" of content. In addition, because of the very few technical barriers to publishing comics, and the medium's flexibility in terms of length (i.e., meaning can be iterated with a single panel), you may find yourself returning to this form of scriptwriting as an effective way to enhance literacy across the disciplines and to assess students' ability to process and respond to content from other media: They can write comics adaptations of everything from Shakespeare to today's headlines.

CHAPTER 4

MOVIE AND TELEVISION SCRIPTS

Explaining why students might love writing television and movie scripts almost seems like a waste of time: Kids live for this stuff. Moreover, they delight in finding out how much they already know about these media but never had a chance to articulate, let alone use as a springboard for their own writing. Also, by writing for moving-image media, students will be able to supplement their experiential prior knowledge with whatever else they already know about scripts, such as those for stage plays or comics.

WHY TEACH THIS?

Ever notice how often we naturally tend to process or convey information in "movie mode"? Young people narrating real-life anecdotes often tell them as if they're dramatic scenes, and, as we get older, our memories look like movies to us. The takeaway here is that thinking in images is arguably a basic state from which we must be trained to learn the conventions of prose text. That's why educators shouldn't see writing for moving-image media as "technology-based" or somehow esoteric when compared with print media. Instead, it combines the concision of writing audio scripts with the visual language of comics and thereby both prepares and reinforces student writing skills across a wide range of texts.

Common Core State Standards for Skills Focus

W.7.3. Write narratives to develop real or imagined experiences or events using effective technique, relevant descriptive details, and well-structured event sequences.

W.7.3d. Use precise words and phrases, relevant descriptive details, and sensory language to capture the action and convey experiences and events.

W.11–12.3. Write narratives to develop real or imagined experiences or events using effective technique, well-chosen details, and well-structured event sequences.

W.11-12.3d. Use precise words and phrases, telling details, and sensory language to convey a vivid picture of the experiences, events, setting, and/ or characters. (NGA Center & CCSSO, 2010, pp. 42–46)

Skills Preview

In this chapter, you will learn to help students do the following:

- Craft descriptive text with vivid sensory imagery, a crucial part of moving-image scripts
- Practice the general narrative maxim "show, don't tell" so that information is presented smoothly (often indirectly) to audiences
- Deepen their understanding of nonprint media and how to read its visual "texts"
- Distinguish between the similar formats but different audiences and purposes addressed by screenplays and teleplays
- Create storyboards that connect the reading strategy of visualization to the start of the writing process

GETTING STARTED

It's hardly ever necessary to motivate young people to talk about moving-image media. However, you may find that they're not as quick to discuss the *writing* on a film or TV series; instead, they may want to discuss memorable characters, a hilarious one-liner, and so on—without acknowledging that these are the natural results of a high-quality script.

Prompt students to reflect on the importance of scriptwriters to movies and TV by having them brainstorm popular titles they've enjoyed and evaluate whether the success of each was due to the screenplay/teleplay or its execution. Encourage students to "dig deeper" and identify the aspects of the script that set the stage for achievement in other, more apparent ways. For example, young viewers may recall an exciting chase scene or the appealing performance by a star, but they may not reflect beyond this surface observation to acknowledge that a writer described the pursuit and composed the dialogue the actor used to create that character.

QuickStart: Transcribe It

Many screenplays and teleplays published in book form are actually transcriptions—a written record of the finished product rather than the plan for it. For this reason, they can sometimes be a bit less interesting for writers to study—they are so cleaned up, and match the finished film so exactly, that they provide an unrealistic impression of how scripts really work.

On the other hand, the *process* of transcribing can be a great learning tool. Simply screen a brief clip, no more than a few seconds long, from a scripted movie or TV show and replay it as needed so that students can describe in writing what they see and hear. You can even have students work together, so they can push each other to make their descriptions that much sharper.

To help them with issues of format, you can provide the model in this chapter for guidance or simply challenge them to figure out the format by having them apply what they may already know about stage plays, radio dramas, and/ or comic book scripts. The beauty of this approach is that they won't be too far off: The formats overlap quite a bit because, as this book argues throughout, there's a common purpose at the core of *any* script, with only the medium changing. Another option is to provide students with a handful of very basic prompts on your board, as shown below, then allow them to suggest replacement text for the placeholders. In essence, a location is described and a single character says one line of dialogue—it's hard to get more basic than that.

```
SETTING OF SCENE
Description of action


                    CHARACTER NAME
                 (delivery directions)
```

If you'd like to extend this activity as a homework assignment, just have students elaborate on the text, in effect transforming their transcript into a script. They can compose "the next 10 seconds" of the story, alter details in the original script, or write a setup scene that precedes the transcripted material.

Learn the Lingo

close-up: A shot in which the camera is near the subject. Scriptwriters specify these only when necessary, and the same is true of extreme close-ups, **medium shots**, and long shots.

cut: The transition between shots in any medium with moving images. If screenplays and teleplays contain cuts at all, they generally specify changes in scenes, not shots.

dissolve: Common in older movies, this is a transition between scenes in which one shot appears to dissolve into the next. This is indicated in a script by the text "DISSOLVE TO:" standing on its own line. (Today this device is much more common in video scripting and editing—see Chapter 5.)

fan fiction: Not a movie or TV term per se, this refers to fiction created by fans as an unauthorized addition to an existing, professionally published or commercially broadcast work. Common in prose form, fan fiction can also surface in the context of videos, comics, and other script formats.

insert: A shot that quickly draws attention to an item before returning to the main action; often used for text that is to be read by the audience such as handwritten notes, newspapers, or wristwatches.

intertitle: A shot displaying text that audiences read in between shots of moving images; sometimes called a "title card" in reference to its use in silent film. The TV series *Frasier* employed intertitles with regularity (and irony).

moving shot: A shot that follows a character while he or she is walking, running, or otherwise actively moving. Indicated simply as "MOVING" in most scripts, it signals that the characters are in motion and that therefore the crew will need to figure out how to move the camera as well.

off screen (O.S.): Similar to "off-panel" in comics and, less so, to "**off-mic**" in audio. This differs from a voice-over; when someone is speaking off-screen, he or she could conceivably enter the viewable space.

pan: A horizontal movement of the camera; short for *panorama.*

shot: A single continuous running of the camera. Screenwriters generally don't have to think in terms of individual shots–that's the job of the cinematographer, editor, and most of all the director–but there are exceptions. If we need to see things in close-up or have specialized shots, such as an "establishing shot" (which briefly conveys a general location from a distance), these should be included in the script.

slugline: A scene heading in a teleplay or screenplay that briefly describes the setting. The time of day is included in sluglines, partly because it needs to be highlighted for production purposes.

two-shot: A shot in which two characters appear at the same time near each other, often in conversation.

webisode: An episode of a web-based "TV series"; typically briefer than a TV episode that would appear on the television platform.

zoom: Diminution of the distance between viewer and subject of a shot through the action of the lens, not by moving the camera closer; used in scripts (sparingly) for sudden emphasis.

Writing for TV and Movies: Leveraging a Cultural Obsession

There are thousands of would-be screen scenarists out there, and there are countless books and seminars that cater to them. For this reason and others, your students may be more interested in these script forms than others, even if they're not yet equipped to follow their professional ambitions. But the key benefits of teaching screenwriting don't just emerge with older students, many of whom will learn and hone their craft, many of them using Joseph Campbell's "Hero's Journey" model to wed psychological and mythological themes to contemporary, commercially informed story structures. To younger students hungry to move to this level, by all means offer them support and encouragement but also point out that a strong foundation in the skills covered in the traditional writing curriculum is crucial to achieving these loftier ambitions.

Make the Connection: Storyboards Across Media

Storyboarding is probably the most powerful prewriting tool in all of scriptwriting—and can help bridge the gap between writing screenplays/teleplays and other script forms with which students are familiar. The term refers to a planning method in which individual shots are illustrated much like comic book panels so that the flow and coherence of the storytelling can be figured out in advance, thus avoiding potential obstacles or delays when shooting actually begins.

Storyboards can be used not just for film and TV, but also, in a tweaked form, for video and digital storytelling (see Chapter 5) as well as some of the projects in Chapter 6. In addition, storyboarding as a skill draws upon the same lessons about visual storytelling that can be learned by scripting comics. (So if you haven't tackled comics yet, this is the perfect way to connect skills going forward, as you can easily segue from storyboarding into sketching page-by-page breakdowns of graphic narratives.)

In the professional world, storyboarding usually comes *after* the script. That's because storyboards are really tools to help directors and cinematographers visualize scenes as a step, and so the scriptwriter is *very* rarely the storyboard artist. However, for student writers, storyboards can be an important aid to the visualization process and help them sequence the events. In short, storyboards are a perfect "graphic organizer" for scriptwriters of screenplays or teleplays.

Although a storyboard is a graphical representation of a scene, it often features handwritten captions or notes to clarify certain details. Storyboarding is particularly helpful for complex sequences. Start by displaying a sample storyboard; examples can be found on both film and artist websites and sometimes on DVDs as extras (see also Appendix A). Allow students some time to examine the storyboard and ask questions about it. Some may immediately remark on its resemblance to a comic or graphic novel. Point out that in storyboards, arrows typically indicate the movement of characters/actors, a device that's not necessary in graphic storytelling since there's no actual movement. (For more details on how students can use storyboards in their scriptwriting, see the prewriting section of this chapter.)

MOVING-IMAGE MEDIA SCRIPT TYPES

Students may have trouble deciding between writing for television and film (if given a choice). The good news is that there is little difference between the script types of screenplay and teleplay in terms of format and, more important, narrative constructive and each medium's formal elements: Most writers, whether professional or beginner, do not have much trouble moving from one to the other. That said, there are some important differences in story structure as well as even more crucial points of commonality that students should keep in mind.

In terms of writing for authentic audiences, it needs to be stated that students simply can't "write for television." If they write a short film, it can potentially be made; and although the odds are against them, students might conceivably see a feature film one day made from their scripts.

In contrast, television is by its nature more series-oriented. Therefore, a single teleplay stands very little chance of ever being produced for the traditional television platform since TV series are generally written by staff writers who work closely with each other and the series' producers or "showrunners." And the odds of creating a brand-new series based upon an individual script are even higher: Producers typically hire writers for such scripting chores (or else they are writers themselves) rather than launching a series based upon unsolicited scripts that writers develop on their own. For these reasons, this section includes information on writing TV sketch comedy and **webisodes**, variations on "writing for TV" that are more feasible in terms of actual production.

Film: Shorts Versus Features

Most screenplays that students will be excited to read and emulate in their own writing will be for feature films—those that run about 90 minutes and that they can see at their local multiplex. However, while using such scripts as mentor texts that can inform storytelling techniques while modeling the professional screenplay format, students would do well to conceive of their own script as one for a short film, the type that screens at film festivals and, often, online.

Nowadays, though, the word *film* in "short film" can be a bit misleading as students can clearly work with each other, as well as filmmakers open to collaboration, to shoot on *video*, which is far easier and much less costly. Indeed, most Hollywood feature films these days are shot and projected via digital video. What you'll want to be aware of is that the skills necessary for scripting short films don't change at all when video *as a production technology* is involved (the video scripts covered in Chapter 5 are a different species), nor do they change much in comparison to feature films. Here's one significant difference regarding the latter, however: Short films usually follow a simplified problem-resolution structure or portray an engaging vignette without the full-blown dramatic development (e.g., in-depth character arcs and constant plot complications/obstacles) upon which feature film scripts are predicated.

Television: Sitcoms Versus Dramas

Students writing teleplays should know that although they can largely approach the script format the same way they might screenplays, the structure of TV scripts is quite different, and additionally varies according to genre and length.

Running about 22 minutes to fit into half-hour slots, sitcoms begin with a teaser that sets up a premise to hook the viewer; it's bookended at the conclusion by a "tag" scene that acts as a dramatic resolution. In between, there are two acts and three commercial breaks. It's possible, of course, that students working in pairs or small groups could write an entire sitcom script, and the satisfaction they derive from this may be worth the necessary coordination of timetables and writing duties.

The key thing for student writers to remember is that, as its name implies, "situation" is of central importance to sitcoms, not one-liners or humorous characters; in that sense, the form echoes the dramatic structure of other texts with which students may be familiar: An inciting incident sets in motion a chain of events characterized by a problem and the attempts of the main character(s) to resolve it. All of the comedy, and character development as well, should arise from those circumstances. The challenge for student writers is that sitcoms rely on the audience's existing familiarity with the characters, their basic relationships with each other, and their foibles. If they are scripting a wholly original sitcom episode, then, the audience has no such prior knowledge, and so establishing this kind of foundation is an extra task that their writing must take on. Of course writing a **fan fiction** teleplay based on a real sitcom is an alternative approach.

The same is generally true of TV drama: The characters, setting, and other cornerstone story elements are preestablished. The difference here is that students can script a pilot episode for a new dramatic series and approach the project as if they were writing a feature film in which not every plot strand needs to be resolved by the ending.

Like sitcoms, TV dramas strategically use a teaser to entice viewers, but often its length and dramatic import is such that it effectively constitutes a miniature act. Three to five additional acts then follow, each except the final one ending on a reveal, reversal, or similar turning point that encourages audiences to stay tuned through the commercials that follow. In short, students should plan 10- to 15-minute "chunks" of action that advance the plot in a substantial way.

What that plot looks like largely depends on whether the TV show is a "procedural" drama or a "series" drama in nature. Nowadays the line between these two categories is often blurred, but it's still worth distinguishing them for students. Series dramas usually spotlight families or communities—what's important are the ongoing relationships between the characters, and outside or intervening events and characters are ultimately important insofar as they impact these relationships. Procedural dramas certainly include ongoing relationships, but they are secondary to the emphasis placed on that week's "case." The case can be an investigative one, a legal one, or a medical one; regardless, the plot points of any given episode hinge on the main characters' progress relative to that case.

Again, the challenge for students in writing a completely original script for either form of TV drama is that there is no preexisting backstory. With this in mind, it may be wiser for students to opt for a procedural episode in that the emphasis can be on the current story and its resolution, without other storylines complicating matters.

However, if students are prepared to take on the challenge of crafting their own TV series from scratch, you may want to work with them by suggesting the webisode format as discussed below. That way they could divide a longer project into what is essentially a series of short films with a recurring cast and more manageable deadlines in terms of writing and producing. In addition, students need not feel compelled to structure their drama into those 10- to 15-minute acts but can make each installment as short as 5 minutes.

TV Sketch Comedy

Sketch comedy may hold appeal for student scriptwriters for several reasons: It's a fun form to collaborate with peers on; the writing product itself is brief and can be performed almost right away; there are multiple platforms for realizing or publishing the final media product (individual video podcasts available for download, streaming webisodes that appear at regular intervals, live performances, or combinations of these). Here are some tips you can provide to students writing these kinds of scripts:

- Decide on a basic type of sketch: pop culture satire, character-driven, product/ad parody, political comedy, and so on. (You may want to screen examples of these different types to help students distinguish between them.) Caution students that comedy writing that does not narrow its purpose and topic runs the risk of straying all over in an opportunistic pursuit of laughs.
- The character names should be listed under a heading for "CAST" at the outset of each script with a number in parenthesis next to it that indicates the total head count. This helps producers and directors make personnel and casting decisions because often several sketches must be developed and rehearsed in the same time period.
- Other than perhaps an initial one, no sluglines should appear in the script, as the action in a sketch should be conveyed in a single scene. The format, then, can resemble that of a short play with a quick "at rise" description of the setting; often this description is introduced with the phrase "LIGHTS on" followed by characters' names, what they're doing, and where they are located.
- Tailor the script to the strengths of its anticipated performers—forcing physical comedy or celebrity impersonations on those whose skill sets aren't a good fit could result in an amusing script but a subpar finished product, which means that as a form of practical writing the script itself is, in the final analysis, subpar.

Webisodes

Sketch comedy, TV drama, and sitcoms can all be conceived and presented as webisodes, for really all that is involved is a change in platform from conventional television to the web. That said, students will need to consider the potential dramatic freedom that such a shift brings during their planning and prewriting, not just when it comes time to "publish." Will their drama in its overall duration reflect the 1-hour slots of television even though they will no longer be constrained by that medium's scheduling parameters? Will their sitcom, when all the individual webisodes are considered, run to the traditional 22 minutes, or will it deviate from television-derived runtimes and that platform's commercial-break-driven structure?

Another important issue students will need to keep in mind concerns continuity, the idea that to the audience the fictional "reality" should seem unbroken. Therefore, even if students are scripting and shooting webisodes over a period of months, the cast needs to wear the same clothing/costumes if, in dramatic time, only a few minutes have passed. Similarly, no one wants to see snow in the background of one scene and then, in a scene taking place the following day in the same location, passersby wearing shorts.

Finally, in practical terms there is little difference between webisodes and video podcasts. Webisodes can be downloaded from existing podcast distribution platforms as well as streamed from a hosting website (such as a school's).

Common Ground: Writing Modes and the Danger of "Overdirecting"

Although writing for the movies and TV sounds glamorous, you'll want to point out that the role of the writer, though critical, is probably more limited than students might imagine when it comes to constructing the visuals. Point out that although in many well-known cases filmmakers write their own movies, it is not the scriptwriter's job to direct the movie or TV episode on the page—meaning, it's not necessary (or professional) to include descriptions of shots and camera angles beyond what's necessary for the basic narrative. In fact, point out to students that it's a sure sign of an amateur when a script is read and earns the criticism that, although the story is fine, the script itself is "overdirected."

To clarify this point, connect it to what students already know about theatrical productions. For example, prompt them to recall the distinction (perhaps based upon personal experience) between a play's director, who may well be a school's drama teacher, and the playwright. Each has a distinct job. Like theater directors, film and TV directors are in charge of the action, guiding actors through each page of the script. However, they also must direct the placement and movement of the camera, shooting each scene until they're pleased with the results.

With these ideas and roles in mind, take time to reinforce the writing modes that writing screenplays and teleplays comprise:

Practical Writing. Like all scripts, screenplays and teleplays are sets of instructions for others to follow—unlike narratives such as poetry or short stories, which represent the end product directly to the reader. Explain that screenplays and teleplays are blueprints: Although the primary audience for these scripts is the director and the actors, other key readers are crew members and producers, the latter being responsible for buying and "developing" scripts in the first place. Remind students that every line of such a script has a practical purpose; it's not just narrative fiction poured into a new format.

Descriptive Writing. Scripts must provide clear and pertinent information about setting (both the time and place of the action), as well as props, wardrobe, and other items that directly bear on the narrative. Again, the scriptwriter's job is not to *be* the costume designer or cinematographer but to provide mission-critical information so that those in such positions can carry out their duties effectively. Students should note, therefore, that brief descriptive passages that create mood and atmosphere *definitely* have their place in screenplays and teleplays; indeed, those who light or score those particular scenes rely on them.

Narrative Writing. A full-length screenplay for a feature film usually follows the rules of dramatic structure that are common to plays and novels (e.g., rising and falling action, climax, and resolution) and also includes the story elements found in other forms of fiction (e.g., characterization, dialogue, setting, pacing). So does the structure of a TV episode, although in both truncated and elongated forms: The dramatic arc of a given episode must unfold more rapidly, whereas character development usually occurs over an entire season—and long-term conflicts are not apt to be resolved in any given episode.

MAKING FRIENDS WITH THE FORMAT

Reproduce and distribute the following script model. Then go over any formatting conventions that are new to students, using the annotations and the Learn the Lingo feature for this chapter as needed.

To demystify things, explain that the format has arisen for real-world reasons, not academic ones or because some authoritative body determined that these are the rules. Likewise, the slight differences between screenplay and teleplay formats reflect the differences in the different production processes and histories of the two media. For example, marking scene numbers and providing a character list at the start of each scene is typical of a format such as a sitcom because the story is put together in a much more modular way and must conform to breaks for commercials (even if the show is on cable—because eventually it must be syndication-friendly on regular broadcast stations). In movies, yes, there are discrete acts, but the structure is embedded in the narrative, more like in a novel. There's no break to signal a new act: It all flows together for the viewer.

Finally, please note that the script format and its conventions are best internalized not just by having students focus on models such as this one but also by studying scripts in conjunction with the finished media products. Then they'll grasp how ideas are "made real." The Guided Viewing activity in Chapter 1 can help in this regard.

FADE IN: ←─── Many screenplays and
                                                            teleplays begin with a "**Fade
EXT. SUBURBAN HOUSE — DAY   ←──────────────   In**" and end with a "Fade to
  ↑   Black."
A school bus pulls up in front of the home to pick
up IDEAL DARRYL, a handsome, athletic-looking 7th-   "EXT." stands for "Exterior"
grader with stylish glasses and clothes.   while "INT." means "Interior."

                    NARRATOR (V.O.)   ←──────   This line of text is called a
              Young Darryl Johnson disliked   "slugline" and describes the
              school. Intensely.   setting. In TV sitcom scripts,
                                                            sluglines appear in all caps
INT. SCHOOL BUS — DAY   and underlined because these
                                                            breaks really need to stand
Ideal Darryl enters the bus and all of the kids   out. In TV scripts for dramatic
become SILENT. Then suddenly CHEERS erupt.   series, which are somewhat
                              ↑   closer to screenplays, sluglines
EXT. SUBURBAN MIDDLE SCHOOL — ESTABLISHING — DAY   are also capitalized but not
                            ↑   underlined.
Throngs of students file in the main entrance.
                                                            Note the difference between
INT. CLASSROOM—DAY   this "voice-over" and the "off-
                                                            screen" dialogue from the
The entire class of students look to Ideal Darryl   Teacher below.
in beaming admiration as he finishes speaking.
                                                            Sound cues appear in all caps
                    IDEAL DARRYL   just as they do in audio scripts.
      ──────→ (smugly)
              . . . and those, in a nutshell, are   A handful of specific types
              all the important ways that a grasp   of shots can be called out in
              of particle physics contributes to   sluglines. Note, however, that
              understanding the causes of the U.S.   screenplays rarely use the actual
              Civil War.   word *shot*—it's understood, so
                                                            omitting it saves space.

                    TEACHER (O.S.)   Brief delivery directions go
              Brilliant, Darryl! You've once again   here, but they should not be
              done a better job of teaching than I   overused. Sometimes these are
              could ever hope to!   called "parentheticals."

                    NARRATOR (V.O.)   Dialogue is indented, as in
              Confused about Darryl disliking   other scripts where actors
              school? Well, you see, that isn't   ←───   must read or memorize their
              Darryl.   lines. Indenting the lines helps
(beat) ←──   them stand out from the rest
              This is.   of the text.

                                                            A "beat" is a measurement of
                                                            time in the performing arts.
                                                            Think of it as a brief pause.

MRS. JOHNSON removes an oversized virtual reality
helmet from her son DARRYL, a smaller, more
disheveled, less confident version of the character
we've already seen. The helmet is connected to
a shelf containing what appear to be boxes of
software. Mrs. Johnson, slightly exasperated,
shakes her finger lightly at Darryl, who appears to
be in a stunned daze.

> Character names appear in all caps the first time they appear in a screenplay or teleplay.

> In a teleplay, personal direction like this appears with the dialogue. In a film script, it's usually written separately. Think of a teleplay as being much more actor- and dialogue-driven, and a film script as more director-friendly and visuals-driven.

          MRS. JOHNSON
     See, that's just what I was afraid
     of. This dream app is too strong
     and too unrealistic for you, Darryl.
     You'll never be able to wake up and
     face the world.

          NARRATOR (V.O.)
     People had lost the ability
     to dream, you understand, and
     were therefore obliged to buy
     prefabricated dream packages.

INSERT — COVER OF DREAM SOFTWARE BOX

> A quick shot away from the action, such as when a character looks at a watch, is indicated this way.

The product title reads "Big Man on Campus—New
Middle School Edition!" and an illustration shows a
silhouetted (and therefore generic) student being
carried triumphantly by faculty and students across
a lawn with a large school building in b.g.

> To save space, this is how the word *background* is abbreviated.

          DARRYL (O.S.)
     Aw, but mom, I don't like the other
     ones. So if we don't buy this one
     I'll be stuck with all my dreams
     from fifth grade all over again!

> Stands for "off-screen."

BACK TO SCENE

> Inserts and **"P.O.V."** **(point-of-view)** shots always return to the main scene with this phrase; there is no need to repeat the original slugline for the scene.

          MRS. JOHNSON
     Oh, no need to worry, Darryl
     sweetie. I think we may still have
     some middle school–appropriate dream
     packages at home to tide you over
     for a spell.

          DARRYL
     Please, Mom, no! I don't want Julia's
     hand-me-downs anymore!

SKILLS FOCUS: "SHOW, DON'T TELL"

As it turns out, the old adage "show, don't tell" applies even more to visual media than to prose. Using examples from class reading as necessary, explain to students that unlike prose fiction, screenplays and teleplays are largely incapable of "telling" directly but rather must relate information by "showing." In TV shows and movies, there simply isn't that omniscient authorial voice to tell us what is going on or that sense of interiority that a well-written short story or novel provides, where we seem to experience everything that the point-of-view character is experiencing from the inside out.

Indeed, this is especially true for personal ideas and feelings in moving-image media. Yes, characters can simply state what they're feeling through dialogue or, in some cases, voice-over, but such devices can quickly seem clunky and contrived to audiences. Instead, dramatic gestures, facial expressions, music, moody settings, and editing techniques are used to suggest psychological states. Invite students to recall other "filmic" ways that movies and TV shows convey emotions, memories, and other inner states. These include "**dissolves**" into flashbacks or dream sequences, subjective camera work, and the expressionistic use of lighting or color.

Such concepts are important, but not because students must use these techniques in their own scriptwriting. Instead, it's more important to emphasize the limited palette of options screenwriters can draw upon to get us "inside a character's head." Otherwise, the temptation for beginning writers is to include text that describes characters as "thinking" about something without realizing that there is no direct way to convey this on screen (one exception is voice-over narration, but it's usually reserved for a single character). Guide students to realize that, in the end, there may not be that great of a difference between scripted texts and prose texts in this respect. Fiction that is capable of presenting actions and feelings for readers to experience vicariously, rather than simply telling them what is transpiring, is generally more effective and a sign of more sophisticated storytelling.

The challenge for scriptwriters is that their scripts must provide sufficient—yet sufficiently open-ended—direction and motivation for actors to use in terms of character development. There's often a fine line, however, between accomplishing this and carelessly trying to indicate interiority directly. For example, you can describe body language and a general tone for a performance: "She slumps when she sees her injured child. She seems to sink into herself and into her misery." Things are left so that the actors can convey this idea through their posture, movements, and vocal inflection. That's different from writing this: "Upon seeing her injured child, she feels that her life has changed irrevocably. She knows that there is no point continuing to fight the evil, that she was foolish even to try."

SKILLS FOCUS: DESCRIPTIVE WRITING

For the same reason that having characters constantly discussing their feelings is not the most elegant way of conveying story information, having them directly describe sense impressions isn't effective either. Instead, good scripts rely on the actions and descriptions of characters to illustrate information and to lead the audience to infer sensory details from the dialogue.

Okay

"That's the smelliest dog I've ever encountered."

Better

(recoiling) "Wow, did someone just drive a garbage truck in here? Wait, who let that dog in here?"

Work with students to brainstorm ways to express sensory details by showing rather than telling. Even the sense of sight might need to be evoked in a screenplay when a character has to react to something off-screen that the screenwriter is not yet ready to reveal to the audience. For example, if a character's gaze travels upward, what does it say about the size or location of the object being viewed? Or if characters shield their eyes, what does that imply about what they're looking at or toward?

To practice descriptive composition in the context of scriptwriting, write the following phrases on the board and have students provide ways of "describing" them using only stage directions, dialogue, sound, visual compositions, and so on. Challenge them individually or in groups to compose the most economical yet most descriptive text possible, and to come up with additional examples.

- Extreme heat
- A fragrant garden
- An itchy wool sweater

As a follow-up activity, ask students to consider how they might write delivery directions (i.e., instructions to the actors for how to deliver lines) with a high level of precision, for this, too, is a type of descriptive writing—one that helps actors and directors do their jobs. Elicit words such as *whispering, wailing, sobbing,* or *barking,* and have students record them in their writing journals for future reference.

Finally, explain that conventions in the screenplay and dramatic teleplay formats are designed to support the "1-minute rule," in which a single page is supposed to correspond to 60 seconds of screen time. In a teleplay for a sitcom, a page equals 30–40 seconds of time. With such space constraints, concision is paramount, and so writers must employ descriptive words precisely and efficiently.

SKILLS FOCUS: SETTING

Setting is often overlooked in movies and TV shows because it is often merely a backdrop against which the flashier elements of character, dialogue, and action play out. At the same time, though, it's a memorable setting that distinguishes movies and TV series from each other, and an effective setting adds to the overall believability, or verisimilitude, of the work. With this in mind, provide the following questions to students as they plan or draft their scripts.

- *What time of year is it?* The amount of light at dinnertime or whether it's still dark out when characters wake in the morning should align with real-world conditions. Can you convey a particular season with small details, such as having holiday decorations appear in a trashcan in the background?
- *What period is your story set in?* The importance of details related to costumes or props can't be overstated. Moreover, make sure the period is as precise as possible. For example, saying "The Middle Ages" or "The Old West" can lead to errors of vagueness down the road. After all, the Middle Ages lasted for centuries, with cultural changes occurring throughout, and the Old West of the prewar Dakotas is quite different from that of 1890s Arizona or California.
- *What is the physical environment like?* Characters shivering and wearing coats can indicate a chilly day even if the film or TV show is shot in the summer, so the script should include such details. Also keep in mind aesthetic factors such as architecture and décor.
- *Are you remembering to use sound?* Audio is a great way to convey setting, but it's sometimes neglected in moving-image media. But consider its impact on a scene that remains unchanged visually. For example, picture a family sitting in a living room—and then add a howling winter wind outside. Or imagine a couple driving in a car and then, suddenly, raindrops begin to pound on the roof . . . or a police siren can be heard approaching them.
- *Are you providing information directly if appropriate?* Convey information explicitly to the audience if necessary. This might seem to violate the "show, don't tell" rule, but not if it's done sparingly. Recall the famous on-screen text scroll that begins the 1977 film *Star Wars*, noting that both components of setting (time and place) are contained in the phrase "A long time ago in a galaxy far, far away."

SKILLS FOCUS: VISUALIZATION

The ability to "think visually" can help inform virtually all student writing, both fiction and nonfiction, as doing so effectively can produce text that allows readers to create their own mental imagery more easily. Invite students to share how they create mental pictures before writing descriptively; some visual learners may even make sketches or diagrams as part of the prewriting process. For these reasons, it's important to convey that scriptwriters think about film and TV stories in "visual chunks," either as shots or groups of shots that can be included under a single scene heading. The goal is to help students grasp that in their own scriptwriting they need to think about visuals not as an afterthought but as a priority—not as replacement for narrative, but as the very way that narrative *works* in moving-image media.

Teachers and students have long been accustomed to comparing and contrasting novels with their big-screen adaptations in terms of narrative content, but students still rarely spend much time learning how to "read" films in their own right, as a medium with its own unique ways of making meaning apart from the script's storyline. Similarly, many adult audiences who watch TV and movies do so passively, not looking too closely at the various elements of a production. How, then, do we help our students use critical-thinking and critical-viewing skills to become active viewers? One way is to teach students about how films are made and to help them understand that films are also a type of text designed to be "read."

Once students have chosen a subject for their script, you can guide them through a visualization exercise regarding a single scene or portion of a scene. To do this, pair them up and then simply have each scriptwriter take turns, with eyes closed, slowly narrating what he or she sees. You can record each pair by using computer mics or a mobile phone with a voice memo feature, so that speakers can play back their own words and incorporate them into prewriting text. Or the partner can take notes that are then shared with the scriptwriter. And this process can be repeated using a gradual-release-of-responsibility model: Eventually students should take notes themselves on what they're visualizing, and they should do so not while listening to a recording but "live," while in the act of creating mental imagery.

Another visualizing activity I recommend is called "Script versus Clip," a more specific form of the Guided Viewing activity in Chapter 1. Simply distribute a page of a teleplay or screenplay (see the Additional Resources section of Appendix A for sources), preferably one that your class is not familiar with but one for which the finished film is available and appropriate for in-class viewing. Read it aloud with your students. Again, note that although published screenplays and teleplays are readily available, they often represent a "cleaned-up" transcription of a popular work, not the original work done by the scriptwriter. To clarify this distinction, point out that the audience for screenplays in book form is different—not those making the film or TV series, but fans who have already seen the completed product.

In order to connect the written page to the clip more powerfully, before viewing, have students make predictions based upon the script. Here are some prompts to get them started:

- What do you think this scene will look like? What details not mentioned explicitly in the script may be present? Will the setting be bright, shadowy, or a mix?
- What do you think this scene will sound like? What ambient sounds or music would be appropriate?
- How do you think the director filmed the action? From what camera angles, points-of-view, and distances?
- What impression will you get of the characters from this scene? Will you like or dislike them as a result?
- What do you think the actors will look like, in terms of both physical appearance and enhancements such as wardrobe and makeup? Which of these aspects do you think the script is responsible for?
- What mood will the scene have? Specifically, which of the previously described elements will contribute to that mood?

After viewing the clip, continue to have students compare and contrast it to the script page. In particular, can they confirm their earlier predictions? The goal here is to shed light on the "space" between print and nonprint text. Probe for understanding by asking questions such as the following:

- What decisions were made that forced the movie to diverge from the screenplay?
- When do you think those decisions were made—while shooting or during the editing process?
- What evidence do you have to support these opinions?

You can support students as they respond to these broad issues by prompting them with more-granular post-viewing questions that force them to recall specifics:

- Could the film clip have been edited differently? If so, how?
- How did the art director and/or production designer evoke the setting of the film?
- How did camera shots communicate meaning? Did they create distance, intimacy, distortion, or some other feeling?
- How did music contribute to the mood of the film, including your sense of how the clip was paced?

- How did sound effects influence your experience of the scene?
- In what ways was lighting used to create dramatic (or subtle) effects?

To focus student viewing, don't hesitate to screen the clip in unconventional ways. For instance, try using the brightness control to black out the image entirely and have students listen just to the dialogue and sound effects. Or try the opposite—have students watch a scene while the volume is muted. Such approaches help students deconstruct the different elements of the medium into what could be called separate "text tracks" that can be read and analyzed separately. What can listeners detect in a tone of voice as distinct from an actor's expressions or gestures? Or how does body language convey emotion apart from the actual words of the script?

Ironically, by breaking down the discrete pathways that a movie or TV show can take in order to provide story elements to the audiences, students can better appreciate how these different channels work *together* seamlessly in the pages of an effective script. For example, the images themselves can convey a present-tense narrative (two heroes are pursued by bad guys in their car) while the dialogue conveys a different set of information about the past (how they got into this mess and who's to blame) and an off-screen sound effect of thunder signals an event in the near future (there will soon be a downpour).

Another technique you may want to experiment with is to have English subtitles displayed on the screen while viewing. This practice can help students get a sense of what the dialogue looks like "on the page" versus how an actor's interpretation "brings it to life." To support verbal/auditory learners or to provide an opportunity for others to practice their listening and speaking skills, invite students to provide alternate line readings of the script than those given by the actors. For English language learners, consider providing the alternate of paraphrasing the lines or ad-libbing additional ones in order to practice oral language skills.

LITERACY ACROSS THE DISCIPLINES: BIOPICS

Want to extend moving-image scriptwriting skills to reinforce curriculum in science, history, and even math? Try having students write a screenplay (or teleplay) for a "biopic" (after perhaps first coordinating an interdisciplinary approach with colleagues).

While the term *biopic* traditionally applies to a full-length film biography, you can have students script one or two important scenes that both portray a dramatic moment *and* accurately convey the relevant content area details. For models of the form, you might screen clips of any number of film depictions of the life of Abraham Lincoln, *A Beautiful Mind* (about mathematician John Forbes Nash), or classic Hollywood biopics of notable scientists (e.g. *Madame Curie*, *The Story of Louis Pasteur*).

To keep the project engaging, point out that technology innovators—perhaps those who pioneered popular games or consumer electronics—are fair game as long as there exists the potential for true *drama*, not just *dramatization*. For example, is there a particularly striking moment of success—a "eureka" scene—or one of disheartening failure? Either way, students will need to gather information by means of research not only into the life of their protagonist but also on period details, both those related to the content areas (e.g., the types of scientific apparatus in use) and those that correspond to the times generally (e.g., what people wore, what expressions they used).

THE WRITING PROCESS

Ideas for Prewriting

Students who want to write feature-length films or even hour-long TV dramas may be disappointed to discover that they probably won't have time to do so as a school assignment—drafting a script of that length (roughly 100 pages for a movie, 70 for a dramatic teleplay) can take weeks, if not months. As an alternative, suggest that students write the opening scenes of a movie or the first act of an hour-long drama; in both cases the results should be around ten script pages.

Some students may express interest in writing a fan fiction–style script for an existing TV series—a practice you might want to encourage because it enables writers to focus on the particular script rather than on creating a fictional world from scratch. As with any form of fan fiction, the writer's prior knowledge as a fan informs the creation of a new story using the same basic "universe" as the existing work. So instead of prohibiting such student writing (in TV, film, or any other script type covered in this book) as marginally plagiaristic, consider encouraging students to maintain continuity with the real show in terms of character, theme, and setting while also investing it with their own emotions, interests, and personal perspective.

If, on the other hand, students opt to write the opening of the pilot of an entirely original series, you may want to assign them additional prewriting mini-assignments such as drafting character bios or a creating a "bible" that provides backstories and other important information (see Chapter 3). Clarify that prewriting on this scale is necessary if one is setting out to create an ongoing fictional world.

If students are creating storyboards as a form of prewriting, guide them to first gather their ideas, perhaps in a series of unconnected sketches. In other words, they should approach the task just as they would the early stages of the writing process even though here they're dealing with images: They should first let their creative juices flow. Only afterward should they vet the results to arrive at the strongest visuals for telling the story they want to tell. In fact, have students identify the key images the audience will want or expect to see given the content—these images are the students' building blocks. Then they can decide how to present the subjects of these shots, paying special attention to the mood they want to create. What basic story information needs to be included in the scene? For example, how are characters acting or interacting and what critical actions and gestures *need* to be shown?

As students work through these questions visually to complete their storyboards, they'll be creating a blueprint of the scene that they can then write. Although the storyboard may end up including much more detail than they'd describe in a script, assure students that it's always better for writers to have too many ideas to work from than too few.

Time-Saver: Repurpose Comics

To expedite students' progression through the prewriting stage, have them use a comics script that they have already created, or even just a set of breakdowns, as the basis for their teleplays or screenplays. In fact, the thumbnails can be enlarged and expanded upon to become a set of storyboards (see the "Make the Connection" activity on storyboard creation). Ask students to think about how they would adapt the visual information for the screen. For example, where could arrows be added to storyboards to indicate in which direction characters are moving, and how might these be related to motion lines in comics?

Also, have students consider that film and television scripts have the same approaches to characterization as in comics: Characters can speak and act, they can be seen as the object of others' speaking and acting, and finally, we can hear about them directly. However, this last option is more awkward in movies than in comics, where a narrative caption is considered less obtrusive than voice-over narration.

Ideas for Drafting

First, let students know that, if they've been using storyboards, they should feel free to alter them as needed during the drafting stage. In essence, allow students to feel inspired to add an extra exchange of dialogue or a striking image that occurs to them once they've begun scripting. Disavowing the entire structure of a sequence is a different matter, though, and they should probably consult with you before going down this path. In general, though, students should feel supported by their storyboards, not constrained by them.

Remind students to keep scenes brief by having the visuals tell the story. Dialogue should be to the point and not convey information that can be handled by other means: Inserting an anxious facial expression into a script can achieve a lot in only a handful of words. Of course this approach is part and parcel of "show, don't tell" (see the Skills Focus for this chapter), but it's also a way to keep the script lean and the pacing on track as well.

Remind students to revisit their conceptions of their scripts' audience and purpose periodically. They should keep in mind, for instance, that if they're writing a TV episode or a film in a given genre, then fans of that genre will have certain expectations. Those writing comedies should make sure that their scripts are not just smart or cute, but are actually *funny*; those writing thrillers must include elements of peril or suspense.

Differentiated Instruction

Advanced Students Can . . .

- Adapt narratives across media, using the story elements from a literary or graphic text in a TV or movie script. Encourage these students to think critically before and during the process—what aspects of their favorite comic or YA series are likely to be lost in the transition, and what might be gained, in turn?
- Apply the terminology of specific "shots" in their scripts just as the professional model in this chapter does. These might include reaction shots, low-angle shots, and so on.
- Describe settings and shot compositions that include items of symbolic or metaphoric meaning; examples might include specific colors or visual motifs with associations to people, ideas, and things beyond those actually in the script.

English Language Learners Can . . .

- Understand the format and conventions of scripts better if you provide additional background information on the TV and film industries as necessary. In the United States, where "entertainment news" is a prominent part of new broadcasts, we almost take it for granted that everyone knows something about how movies and TV shows are made, but actually this varies from culture to culture.
- Maximize the benefit they get from any clips you show in class if you first activate the closed-captioning option or, if available, subtitles in their native language. If that distracts native English speakers, you can screen clips twice, once with and once without captions, or prescreen them with ELLs, who can then view the captionless version with the rest of the class as their second viewing. This way, they (and you) can focus on language and vocabulary issues on the first viewing and on script- and media-related issues on successive ones.
- Give a dramatic reading of an excerpt from a teleplay or screenplay. Coach ELLs so that the meaning of delivery and stage directions (e.g., *interrupting*) are clear, and encourage them to rehearse multiple line readings, experimenting with different dramatic interpretations of the text each time. Of course for this and other performance-based activities you will be able to gauge best which students are more comfortable listening for a while before speaking themselves.

- Provide a verbal walk-through of their storyboards for you or other students. By using this oral language approach, scriptwriters can start to identify the vocabulary necessary for drafting their scripts before actually sitting down to do so.

Below-Level Students Can . . .

- Activate their prior knowledge about a closely related script form, stage plays. Help them identify commonalities such as stage directions, delivery directions, and scene breaks.
- Adapt works that they have already written for your class or for another class. That way they can repurpose everything from dialogue to facts that they've already researched, allowing them to focus instead on story structure, their script's descriptive passages, and so on.
- Benefit from your downplaying all the details involved in proper script formatting. Instead, they should focus on audience and purpose, realizing that if they do so even an imperfectly formatted script can be clear and functional.
- Get support navigating screenplay format by relying more heavily on storyboards as a form of scaffolding. Although all storyboards have some text in the form of notes, students can amplify these by adding snatches of dialogue and other story elements. In this way, they'll start to develop the content of their script and become less daunted by the prospect of dealing with format issues simultaneously.
- Engage in "reverse storyboarding" to help them better understand how scriptwriters structure, pace, and visualize scenes or even entire scripts. Simply start with a page or two from a professional script and have students turn it into a storyboard—but not one that matches the final film version. By acting like directors in this way, students will come to appreciate what makes for a good script, namely, clarity of writing and a strong visual organization.

Ideas for Revising

Point out that screenplays and teleplays for pilots are subject to a long and often intensive revision process before they become "shooting scripts." TV scripts for recurring series also have revision periods, but these periods are apt to be briefer and involve fewer major changes. Such shows are often developed by writing teams in addition to having specific writers for individual episodes.

With these professional models of process in mind, consider incorporating some team-based peer editing into the revision stage; for example, a select group of readers can submit feedback memos to the scriptwriter or hold roundtable discussions in which they provide supportive critiques that the writer is free to use or not.

Remind students that they should follow the screen-time-per-page rule of their chosen format (again, 60 seconds for movies and hour-long dramas, 30–40 seconds for sitcoms). If their scripts do not conform to this guideline, what adjustments will they have to make?

Reproduce and distribute the Movie and Television Revision Checklist in Appendix B. Advise students to refer to these as they strengthen their scripts through revision. You can also share the Movie and Television Scripts rubric in Appendix C.

WRAP-UP

With moving-image media such as film and TV, unlike with audio and graphic narrative media, it's easy for the value of *words* to become lost in the primacy of the visual. This chapter has shown how writing for film and TV can instead be used to heighten awareness of the power of word choice, especially when it comes to making narratives more vivid. Moreover, students who undertake to write such scripts develop a keen awareness of the parallel text tracks that operate in such multimodal media, as when an image may be saying one thing while the dialogue may be conveying quite another meaning. In this way, students can also gain a from-the-inside-out understanding of how these media sometimes position them as spectators in ways about which they had previously been unaware, a key component in enhancing critical literacy.

CHAPTER 5

DIGITAL STORYTELLING AND VIDEO SCRIPTS

Writing scripts for video or digital storytelling will strike many students as more of an art project—or even a game—than a writing assignment. However, perhaps even more than when writing movie scripts, students will need to "think visually" throughout the composition process and pair this approach with sensitivity to audio components such as music and spoken word. Moreover, the production aspect is even more closely intertwined with the writing than other types of scripts: Those who write videos and digital stories are often, if not usually, the same people who make the finished product. For these reasons, it's possible that students may not even notice all the writing skills they can hone through these scripts—they'll be too busy enjoying themselves.

WHY TEACH THIS?

Writing video and digital story scripts represents a new vehicle for practicing essential skills from research and expository writing to delivering oral presentations and visual literacy. The range of potential writing tasks coupled with an intuitive format and, thanks to current technology, an easier-than-it-looks production path make the classroom applications quite appealing—which helps explain why these media have seen an explosion in popularity in schools in recent years. In addition, think of scriptwriting for them as an important opportunity to engage in multimodal learning (see this chapter's Make the Connection) and you'll discover that such scripts allow students to create media products that both authentically engage their outside-of-school literacies and are personally meaningful to them (Miller, 2010). Enhanced visual and media literacy skills that can then be transferred to other texts, even print ads, are just an extra bonus.

Common Core State Standards for Skills Focus

W.7.9. Draw evidence from literary or informational texts to support analysis, reflection, and research.

W.7.1. Write arguments to support claims with clear reasons and relevant evidence.

W.7.7. Conduct short research projects to answer a question, drawing on several sources and generating additional related, focused questions for further research and investigation.

W.7.8. Gather relevant information from multiple print and digital sources, using search terms effectively; assess the credibility and accuracy of each source; and quote or paraphrase the data and conclusions of others while avoiding plagiarism and following a standard format for citation.

W.7.6. Use technology, including the Internet, to produce and publish writing and link to and cite sources as well as to interact and collaborate with others, including linking to and citing sources.

SL.7.5. Include multimedia components and visual displays in presentations to clarify claims and findings and emphasize salient points.

W.11–12.9. Draw evidence from literary or informational texts to support analysis, reflection, and research.

W.11–12.1. Write arguments to support claims in an analysis of substantive topics or texts, using valid reasoning and relevant and sufficient evidence.

W.11–12.7. Conduct short as well as more-sustained research projects to answer a question (including a self-generated question) or solve a problem; narrow or broaden the inquiry when appropriate; synthesize multiple sources on the subject, demonstrating understanding of the subject under investigation.

W.11–12.8. Gather relevant information from multiple authoritative print and digital sources, using advanced searches effectively; assess the strengths and limitations of each source in terms of the task, purpose, and audience; integrate information into the text selectively to maintain the flow of ideas, avoiding plagiarism and overreliance on any one source and following a standard format for citation.

W.11–12.6. Use technology, including the Internet, to produce, publish, and update individual or shared writing products in response to ongoing feedback, including new arguments or information.

SL.11–12.5. Make strategic use of digital media (e.g., textual, graphical, audio, visual, and interactive elements) in presentations to enhance understanding of findings, reasoning, and evidence and to add interest. (NGA Center & CCSSO, 2010, pp. 42–46)

Skills Preview

In this chapter, you will learn to help students do the following:

- Respond to literature by scripting book trailers and video poetry
- Enhance research skills such as evaluating and citing sources by writing nonfiction scripts

- Write effective PSA scripts by structuring them like problem-solution essays
- Practice writing in the expository and persuasive modes by scripting news spots and commercials
- Learn how writing news spots must answer the "5Ws plus an H" questions that audiences will have: *Who? What? Where? When? Why? How?*

GETTING STARTED

At this point, you may be wondering, what exactly *are* video scripts—and why does this chapter pair them with digital storytelling scripts in the first place? Aren't TV shows and even most movies shot on video these days? And wasn't that covered in the previous chapter?

To keep things simple, we'll be calling anything that is *compiled*—either from original or preexisting footage and materials—a "video" or a "multimedia presentation." Scripts for these types of videos can function as *instructions* to shoot new video footage (see the sample script in the QuickStart activity), and one could even use a multimedia presentation script to plan the original shots necessary to produce the finished product (video would then just be one of the media used). When these types of video scripts indicate speech, it does not refer simply to narration of some sort—it's typically from a recorded sound bite or an interview that was shot expressly for the production—in other words, the responses are not scripted. Movies and TV shows, by contrast, are literally *pre*-scriptive: People only say what the scriptwriter has decided they will.

Building on this concept is digital storytelling, a slideshow-style "movie" assembled out of preexisting digital assets. Unlike movie or TV scripts, the raw materials of such digital storytelling scripts are usually photos, artwork, music and other audio files, modest clips of original **animation**, and (somewhat more rarely) existing video. Using software such as iMovie, Movie Maker, or Photo Story, digital storytellers can record voice-over narration to images they have downloaded (from the Internet) or uploaded (from a classroom computer or camera). It's really that simple.

QuickStart: On-Air Promos

What type of TV commercial do people watch more than any other? The answer, perhaps surprisingly, is ads for *other* TV shows called "**on-air promos**." These commercials also happen to embody the notion of "video" because they depend mostly on existing footage from the actual shows, with new voice-overs or print graphics added to shape the message and persuade viewers to watch the telecast being promoted. On-air promos also need to be brief, with durations of 5, 10, 15, 30, or 60 seconds.

Ask students to think about their favorite television show. How could they persuade others to watch a summertime rerun of an episode that the students themselves have already seen but which the target members of the viewing audience have not? Provide a two-column (T-chart-like) script template with the heads "Video" and "Audio" (see the model that follows or the annotated one later in the chapter) and have them fill in the video column with descriptions of clips they think would sell the show. Any dialogue as well as voice-over narration should go in the audio column. Additional graphics, such as text that tells when the episode will air, should go in the video column. Supply prompts with phrases typical of on-air promos:

- Next time on . . .
- Ever wonder how . . . ?
- Will X do Y . . . ? Or will A do B . . . ? (a device called "the unanswered question")
- The moment the nation has been waiting for . . .

Students who are not fans of any particular TV series can have the option of writing a promo for an upcoming sports broadcast. Or, if you'd like to use the idea of writing a promo without tying it directly to television content, have students compose a parody of one that promotes a real-life event, as the script shown here does.

On-Air Promo for Geology Class   1

VIDEO	AUDIO
Closed door to classroom	Music: low chord, rumbling and ominous
Door suddenly swings open	Narrator: Next time in geology class . . .
Close-ups on student faces, some anxious	Narrator: Will everyone pass the pop quiz? Who will survive . . .
Broken pencil tossed into a trashcan	Narrator: . . . and who won't?
Text on screen: Geology, Third Period, M-F.	Narrator: Geology—don't miss the excitement.

Make the Connection: Multimodal Storytelling

As its name would imply, in digital storytelling scripts it's story that drives everything, and it largely takes the form of audio narration; the same can sometimes be said of video scripts, but more often audio and visual work hand in hand. By contrast, in digital stories the images are clearly selected to *support* the narrative. Still, what's worth noting is the degree to which there are two separate modes of information—one could even call them separate "tracks" of text.

In fact, in all the media covered in this book so far, with the sole exception of audio scripts, ideas are expressed along more than one pathway. That's different from reading print text or listening to pop music, and this is a difference worth calling attention to. Indeed, you can enhance students' ability to "read" a range of media, from movies to comics, by guiding them in analyzing the ways that these multiple text tracks team up in telling a story.

Which is the primary track, if there is one? What makes it the primary track? Moreover, what is the exact role of the second one at any given point? Does it simply reinforce the first message, or does it clarify it, add fresh information, or even offer a contrasting message? By asking questions like these about multimodal texts, students will become more sophisticated readers—and writers—of texts not only like the scripts covered in these pages but also of everything from print ads to web pages.

Almost oddly, by focusing on how different modes work together, you may discover that what results is an enhanced appreciation of each respective track or medium's strengths. And by making this a recurring conversation when writing for media, you'll be helping students transfer the insights they learn in one medium to any new one to which they subsequently turn.

Learn the Lingo

In addition to reviewing the below terms for students, you may want to revisit the lingo for movies and TV in Chapter 4, as many of those terms are frequently used in video and digital storytelling production–and vice versa.

ambient sound: Background sound recorded live; a type of **SOT** (see *SOT*, this list). It can help establish a setting or set a mood. However, eliminating it also allows greater clarity for voice-over, music, or sound effects.

animation: Any image that is presented as moving when it does not in fact move (not simply what commonly might be thought of as a "cartoon"). Slideshow applications, for example, typically enable users to create very simple animations of text to use for multimedia presentations. Students should know, though, that if animations do not fit their audience and purpose they can be seen as gimmicky and distracting.

A-roll: Footage consisting of interviews, documented events, and images tied to specific script content and critical points that need to be covered or expressed visually. A-roll is the most important video footage that can be used in a finished video or in a multimedia production.

beauty shot: Stunning but nonessential image that adds visual appeal to a video. These shots can range from scenic vistas to flowers in a shop window.

B-roll: Footage that can be used as filler or for transitions. B-roll is more generic in its relationship to the subject matter than A-roll. However, often B-roll images are visible over A-roll audio (e.g., key quotes frequently taken from an interview) as a way of illustrating the audio content instead of simply showing the speaker on camera as a so-called "talking head."

dissolve: A transition whereby a shot replaces another by fading out while the other fades in; in video editing, this can easily be done with effects.

graphic: Any still image, art, or text used in a video or a multimedia presentation.

over-the-shoulder shot: Shot composed as if standing right behind someone, usually a speaker in a conversation or interview.

platform: The physical means by which media products are disseminated. For example, film is a medium but movies can be delivered by broadcast, Internet streaming, DVD, or theatrical projection—all different platforms.

POV: Short for "point of view"; a shot that seems to be subjective, meaning that the camera is used as a surrogate for the vision of someone who appears on screen.

SOT: Short for "sounds on tape"; distinct from sound that is not captured as part of the videotaping process, such as voice-over narration or added music. Often SOT is used independently of the video images that were recorded with it. Pairing SOT with different images can create interesting contrasts or grab the viewer's attention in novel ways.

spec: To provide specifications (a detailed description) for a piece of media to be created or to be identified and supplied if it already exists.

voice-over: Audio narration laid on top of images by a speaker removed from the action.

wipe cut: A cut achieved by one image/shot wiping away and replacing the previous image; a common video effect.

DIGITAL STORYTELLING AND VIDEO SCRIPT TYPES

Before introducing discrete script types such as a PSA or video poetry, you'll want to make sure that students grasp the distinction between such scripts and those in Chapter 4. Share either of the two-column video scripts in this chapter, explaining that while, yes, we're still dealing with moving images, these are *not* filmed dramatic works. Point out how pared-down the video scripts are by comparison, and that there are no complex interactions between characters or dialogue. Instead, the purpose of such scripts is to pair audio and visual elements, supplying transitions as needed. Consider inviting volunteers to explain the kinship with digital storytelling, which also depends on assemblage.

But what about when it comes to choosing between video and digital stories? Your chief decision regarding students in this respect is the degree to which you want them to call for the production of brand-new media artifacts. Are there really the time and skill set necessary for shooting extensive original footage? Still, with today's emphasis on technology integration across the curriculum and the availability of increasingly easy-to-use recording devices, many schools are finding that there are no longer big hurdles preventing the incorporation of video into classroom work. If the script calls for the shooting of original documentary- or news-style footage, writers could approach it as part of the "gathering information and details" stage of prewriting.

Alternately, they could generate original footage through a completely separate writing process that acts as a precursor assignment to the video (or digital story) script itself. Steps in this process might include drafting interview questions or storyboarding/outlining the content of this raw video content, but not necessarily scripting anything *per se*. Alternately, if brief dramatic-style sequences are to be included in scripts (e.g., suppose the anxious actors, playing geology students, in the QuickStart's on-air promo briefly exchanged whispered dialogue with each other), you'll want writers to rely on the skills covered in Chapter 4.

To clarify, though, this chapter deals mostly with scripts with all the elements already present or easily obtainable. Note, for example, that in the on-air promo model, the shots of the classroom door and the student faces need not be recorded as moving images—still photos or drawings can work just as well. The focus here is on writing a coherent script that creates an effective media message, not on how to collect or produce all the individual pieces that might be involved.

So it's up to you to choose how you ultimately want students to use these scripts. Many English language arts teachers work with technology and media departments at their schools on video and digital storytelling productions; others use technology integration funds in the school or district budget to bring in local nonprofits and youth media centers to teach students how to shoot video, conduct on-camera interviews, create digital stories using free multimedia assets, and so on. This chapter's goal is just to give you a sense of the fruitful ways that such activities can not only support your writing curriculum but also provide engaging "21st-century" alternatives to the print-literacy assignments you already use.

Personal Narratives

Digital storytelling is most frequently approached as a form of personal narrative—the writer is also the narrator and the story told is not just personal in that it involves individual history but, usually, in that it relates some kind of autobiographical turning point or special moment. Students then draw or create media artifacts, and/or borrow ones from family members or friends, and supplement these with files they import from other sources.

The end result can be powerful, as it combines authentic student voices with media that are not only engaging but often highly professional. If you decide to assign such a project, here are some suggestions in addition to the ones that can be found in the Writing Process section and elsewhere in the chapter:

- Writing memorable digital stories requires a variety of skills, many of which are addressed earlier in this book. The efficiency that the medium demands—one cannot dwell on a single image for too long—means that using precise language (Chapter 2, Skills Focus: Word Choice) is important. So is an understanding of how to make words and pictures work together when one has a limited canvas on which to combine them (QuickStart Follow-up: Running out of Real Estate, Chapter 3).
- Digital stories are essentially monologues in which the speaker is not visible, but plenty of other images are. For this reason, you may want to incorporate elements of scripting that form (Chapter 1) into your digital storytelling instruction. Similarly, Chapter 2's Skills Focus: Speaking and Listening may contain some valuable tips for students that you will want to consider introducing or revisiting, as the case may be.
- Remind younger students that personal artifacts from earlier in their lives may not be digitized and that, if doing so is not feasible or is too time-consuming, they may want to spec different media items to tell their personal stories.
- Use the section on conducting interviews that appears later in this chapter to encourage greater self-reflection during the prewriting stage, or as a form of peer editing during the revision stage. Simply have students rotate through a series of two or more partners who interview them about the topic of their personal narratives. The interviewers can ask basic, factual questions that indicate to the scriptwriters the kind of information an audience might expect. They can also ask about how certain incidents or events made the writers feel, or how their lives or the lives of others may have changed as a result of those experiences. If the interviews take place at the revision stage, a reading of the draft script can prompt questions such as "Why did you select that particular image (or piece of music)? What meaning does that media hold for you?"

Public Service Announcements (PSAs)

There are numerous benefits to scripting a public service announcement, or PSA, as either a video or a digital story (scripting one for audio is covered in Chapter 2). It can reinforce thematic or social issues in reading and literature and connect to interdisciplinary topics—all while providing a terrific vehicle for persuasive writing.

Start by providing an array of possible issues that students care about to help them choose a writing topic. To connect this media product squarely to your writing curriculum, consider having students practice composing problem-solution-style essays by writing one in script form as a PSA, or have them adapt an existing essay into a PSA. In any case they should consider whether their topic has a strong visual "hook" that comes to mind, as the success of a script will disproportionately hinge upon this (for scriptwriting for audio PSAs, see Chapter 2).

PSAs typically follow the following organization:

- *Attention-grabber:* striking image or sobering statistic
- *Scenario:* illustrates an unpleasant situation or condition, often through a dramatic scene that shows the problem being addressed; it might end on either an upbeat or downbeat note. Bear in mind that students should script the scenario separately, formatting it like a short film so that actors can learn their lines and rehearse the scene or scenes that need to be shot. Then, once video footage exists, they can fold the video and its components into the standard two-column format (see the Making Friends with the Format section) so together you can evaluate the flow and impact of the scenario relative to the rest of the PSA. If it is part of a digital story, the narrator simply recounts the story; images of people need not even appear, as a setting or an object might more powerfully convey a key aspect of the scenario when combined with a voice-over that appeals to the emotions.
- *Call-to-action:* text or narration that tells audience members what they can do in reaction to what they've just seen; sometimes this can come last, after the tagline. The call-to-action must represent a direct or indirect solution to the problem presented at the outset: The audience is asked to take concrete steps themselves or to support a group that is taking such steps.
- *Tagline:* a memorable catchphrase or slogan that can neatly encapsulate the call-to-action, brand an organization, or remind viewers of the gravity of the situation

The initial sections of the script, including the attention-grabber and the first part of the scenario (or the entire scenario if it has a downbeat ending), should lay out the problem for viewers. Relevant supporting facts and statistics should be presented. Then a clear solution should be offered and possibly even dramatized as the conclusion of the scenario section. The call-to-action then explicitly tells viewers how they can be part of that solution. Both the call-to-action and the tagline should blend elements of persuasive writing—memorable and impactful language, a reminder of how the issue might personally affect the audience and its community, an emphasis on how easy it is to take action—with the more dispassionate approach of a problem-solution text.

Commercials and Ads

TV-style commercials share many of the same characteristics as PSAs: They often include a scenario and a tagline and are obviously persuasive in nature. They share brevity as well, with maximum durations of 60 seconds, which runs to one to two pages of script.

Although commercials might seem an odd choice for English composition, consider that the best commercials feature humor, concision, and a keen sense of audience and purpose. Crafting a video or digital story script for a commercial also allows students to practice the skills of persuasive writing.

Here are some other tips and suggestions related to this writing product:

- Caution students to be aware of hyperbole and making exaggerated claims for the product or service they are advertising–unless they are doing so as a form of humor or irony. (You might even want to use this topic as a springboard for discussing ethics and responsibility more generally in writing.)
- Use the topic of commercials to drill down deeper into the concept of writing for an audience. Specifically, ask students to identify the "target audience" for their video. What is the demographic? What is important to that segment of the population? Once scriptwriters have answers to these sorts of questions, they can make more refined decisions regarding word choice and imagery. If time permits, you can enhance students' understanding of audience–and motivate their writing–by having them script ads that sell the same product to different audiences.
- Introduce students to the notion of "See Dog, Say Dog." This refers to the idea that when a voice-over narrator says, "Buy new Ultra-Dazzle laundry detergent today!" we actually see a clear shot of a bottle of Ultra-Dazzle laundry detergent. At key moments in a sales pitch like this, the goal is to have the brand imprint itself on the viewer; if it's presented both verbally and visually, so much the better. In fact, the concluding shot or tagline of many commercials features not just "See Dog" and "Say Dog" but "Write Dog" as well, since text with the brand name often appears on screen, too.

News Spots

News spots are brief video segments that, when combined, can add up to a news broadcast. News spots can also be published as video podcasts, either as stand-alones or as a segment in a longer news magazine in video form. Like documentaries, news spots usually rely on combinations of voice-over, moving images, graphics, and on-camera speakers to cover a topic adequately and engagingly. Like print journalism, broadcast journalism (a category under which video news spots belong regardless of how limited its audience might be), follows a few basic rules for reasons of both informational clarity and ethics:

1. Scripts need a clear "lead" (spelled "lede" in newspaper journalism) that spells out the main issue and provides a dateline (time plus location), the nonfiction equivalent of establishing setting.
2. Reporters and scriptwriters must stick to facts. When opinions are offered, they should be attributed to someone, preferably a person who's obviously credible.
3. Newswriting must answer the "5Ws plus an H" questions that audiences will have: *Who? What? Where? When? Why? How?* Students may want to consider organizing their scripts based upon the order that they answer these questions. You can also encourage them to include at least one piece of media (other than having a news reader simply recite text) that brings each of their answers to these questions to life—an establishing shot, a graphic that spells out the time and date of an upcoming event, and so on.
4. Writers need to structure information like an inverted pyramid. That is, they need to give the "broad strokes" first, eventually working their way to more granular details toward the end of the script.
5. The tone, though conversational, should err on the side of formality, and not include expressions or a tone that is overly familiar or personal.
6. Text should avoid conscious **bias** and the slanted presentation of facts; these are good things for scriptwriters to try to identify during the revision process.
7. Scripting decisions will inevitably shape the news for the audience, so writers should bear in mind that what might seem like even a minor detail (so minor, in fact, that it's left out of the script!) can have a subtle impact on what others perceive as the "truth."

In addition, here are some other ideas and issues to keep in mind when students are scripting news spots:

*   Remember, there are usually two stages to this kind of writing. Students will need to draft any interview questions and plan what kind of images they need to capture on video. They can begin drafting a two-column script (see the Making Friends with the Format section) only after they have these "ingredients" in place.
*   Have writers script narration, which can be read by a student reporter or off-camera anchor if the news spot is part of a longer piece. As an alternative, they can have an on-camera "news reader" read directly from the script. In either case, the tone and voice of the spoken text should be the same.

- Students should think about the graphics that could support the topic they're reporting on. Should they create a diagram, chart, or map? Also, might still images suffice when video footage would be hard to shoot, thus broadening the possible topics that the scripts can cover?
- A great way to teach news literacy is to encourage students to think about whom they want to read their news copy, or simply whom they envision or "hear" reading it when they're drafting it. Is the reader or voice narrator male or female, young or old? Why? What does he or she look or sound like, and again, why? Once students uncover their assumptions about what constitutes an "authoritative" news voice, they can question these assumptions and perhaps bring greater creativity to the task.

Video Poetry

Students can create video poetry, which pairs verse with images and sounds, based upon their own poetry or someone else's. For the latter, students might want to consider using biographical or geographical elements that show the poet and where he or she lived or worked. For the former, writing these scripts can be a vital part of a creative-writing unit. In fact, when video poetry focuses on a student's own work, you can bypass conventional composition or combine it with scriptwriting. In other words, students can draft poetry *directly* into a script template, an approach that might be particularly helpful with visual or auditory learners: They can focus first on how to use what the audience sees and hears to evoke specific feelings, and then, as a second step, compose the actual poetry.

Imagery and Media. Visualization—concentrating on the imagery and sensory details poets want to evoke for their audience—is a natural part of writing poetry. The only difference is that multimedia composition makes the visual and aural aspects of poetry more explicit. The process that many poets and other creative writers can do in a single intuitive leap—experiencing imagery and emotions internally and then capturing them through precise language—can now be broken down into steps that are tangibly "external." For example, a student trying to capture a particular texture or contour with words might now have a photo or piece of art that they can use as a reference or prompt in order to reach a greater precision of language.

As a term, *video poetry* can be tricky since it seems to put an emphasis on scripting an original video. Certainly, writers can take this approach and use the two-column format (see the annotated news spot script in the Making Friends with the Format section), placing the text of the poem (which need not be original) in one column and descriptions of the corresponding images/shots next to it. In this way, the poem being recited becomes illustrated, either in a literal or impressionistic way.

Camera or Computer? Students should also know that actually shooting video, or even using moving images at all, is not a requirement of video poetry. Instead, they can write a script for a digital presentation. When it's produced, still photographs, artwork, text-on-screen, and other graphics can be combined with narration and music to bring the poem to life.

That's not to say that video footage can't be included in such a script—Movie Maker, for example, is considered video-editing software, and "adding videos" is a command just like "adding photos" is. If the goal is to have students shoot video at some point or at least write a script for doing so, that should be considered a subproject: If the media product is heavily skewed toward moving-image video, then it might be best to conceptualize the assignment as purely video from the beginning and do away with still images except for maybe when the title or other text-on-screen is required. Similarly, if the visuals (whether moving or still) seem like anemic accompaniments to the voice-over and music, students might as well write an audio script for recorded poetry (see Chapter 2) and *really* focus on the spoken word aspect.

The easiest way for students to approach writing a script for video poetry is to break the text into chunks and place them in order in the audio or narration column of the script. Sometimes these chunks will correspond to line breaks or stanzas, but often they won't, and students will need to decide how to group ideas and images. Once scriptwriters have mapped out the poem in this way, they can begin the process of assigning visuals to fit each line of spoken audio.

Creative Options. More adventurous students may want to eschew the spoken-word element altogether and see if they can put the emphasis on the power of the poem's text itself. To do this, they need only place that text in the video or image column (which you'll recall is used for anything that is not audio). That way, lines of poetry will appear on screen at intervals for viewers to read silently to themselves, an experience enhanced by the accompanying music, sound effects, and images (either moving or still). In other words, the audience experience would be like that in other forms of video poetry, except it would lack a voice-over narrator reading the poem aloud. In addition, the on-screen text itself can be dressed up with graphics and animation that match the content and voice of the poem. For still images, there are many websites and CD-ROM resources that contain clip art and photos for free use, especially for educational purposes. And of course students are free to create their own artwork, either digitally or by hand, and then have the results scanned.

It's up to you at what stage students should focus on gathering and selecting these pieces of media: They can spec items on a draft of the script as a wish list, or they can gather all their media before even mapping out the text in the audio column—the media pieces themselves may inspire students to organize and present the poem in a certain way. As with all video and digital story scripts, you can have students make a "**paper edit**" of the materials before actually expending the time and effort to find them. Although this stage is simply a form of revision in the media industry, the word *paper* is used to distinguish it from cuts that are actually made to the finished product. A paper edit allows a producer or other collaborator to decide on the individual pieces of media, shots, or audio voice-over that should be excluded or altered before someone goes through the trouble of actually gathering or creating those items.

Digital Storytelling on the Fly

Are you still concerned about the technology involved in creating multimedia presentations? A handy way of engaging students quickly and painlessly involves using a standard slideshow application such as PowerPoint. It comes with a recording feature that allows users to provide an oral narration of the slides. (Some computers have a microphone built in, including most Macs, but if your computers don't, you can easily connect an inexpensive microphone). As UCLA's Jeff Share (2009) demonstrates, students can create their own images that can be photographed with a digital camera, then uploaded and imported into their slideshows. Knowing that they can script and produce digital stories in as little as a single class period is tremendously motivating to students. And bear in mind that this approach works not only for video poetry but also for original narratives, persuasive pieces such as PSAs or book trailers, and even expository texts such as scripts for news spots. In all these cases, keeping the technology simple and accessible allows you—and students—to focus on the writing and the media content.

MAKING FRIENDS WITH THE FORMAT

Reproduce and review the model of the standard two-column video script that follows. This script's genre is a news spot, in this case about an event that's typically held at many schools, a celebration of world cultures in which various projects are presented.

The key point to underscore when analyzing such scripts is that they can be deceptively writer-friendly. On the one hand, they seem "simplified" in format when compared with film and TV scripts. On the other hand, these scripts force the scriptwriter to function more as a director, producer, and/or film editor and require a great deal of thought. Indeed, many writers of video scripts wear one or more of these hats, and the universality of the aforementioned industry practice of the paper edit speaks to the writer's multiple skills and responsibilities.

International Night at Madison School   1

Video	Audio
Title graphic	Ambient[1] SOT[2]: Busy sounds of multipurpose room, with laughter, music, crowds, and so on.
Establishing: parents and kids file into school	Narration: Were you there on the night of January 10th? Madison School celebrated its 8th annual International Night.
Wide shot and pan of multipurpose room, showing all the displays and activities	Principal[3] Charlene Myers welcomed the Madison community, which turned out in record-breaking numbers.
cont.[4]	Principal Myers[5]: It is our privilege to welcome you tonight—thank you for coming out on this cold night. We're very proud of what our students have created. They all worked very hard.
Principal Myers speaking to group	Now, without further ado, I invite you to enjoy all the art, all the informational displays, and most of all . . . the food!
Montage of different ethnic dishes: empanadas, spring rolls, quesadillas, dumplings, and so on	Narration[6]: Boy, she wasn't kidding! One of the great things about International Night is all the cool, tasty foods from around the world you get to sample.
Kenny Wan's mom giving Cindy a sticky rice cake; she tastes it and smiles	Mrs. Wan: This is a sticky rice cake. They're very popular at Chinese New Year, which is coming up soon.
Shots of flamenco dancers in action[7]	Narration: But let's not forget the music. If you ate too much, there was always dancing.
cont.	Music (SOT): Spanish flamenco music

1. Ambient sound makes viewers feel like they're there and helps establish atmosphere.

2. Note how the script is using only the audio track of the video that was shot; the visual here is the title of the work but the festive sounds heard with it create viewer interest. (By the way, SOT = "sounds on tape.")

3. Since there is no audio source identified with a colon, it means that the same source continues, in this case the narrator.

4. This abbreviation indicates that the same visual continues.

5. When someone starts speaking, the script does not automatically show the person. Clarify that it's typical of video storytelling to have audio and video not in perfect sync so that one can help introduce or support the other. Here it's more important to match what the principal is talking about—all the things the students have made—with a visual than to show the principal herself.

6. The job that the narration performs here is typical: point out how it provides a bridge between the different video elements that were shot during International Night.

7. There aren't too many visual details in this script, just general descriptions. Many producers and directors prefer this so that they can select the precise video clips that they want. Other scripts might be more precise here, especially if the writer is also the producer.

Now, what about digital storytelling scripts? Simply put, there is no universally established format for them. This is partly due to the newness of the medium and the brevity of the form (many digital stories run only about a dozen images over 2 or 3 minutes)—it's been easy for practitioners, including educators at various levels, to come up with a script template that fits the needs of specific projects or writers. That's pretty straightforward. But there's also a deeper truth, one that you'll want to share with students, especially if you've framed scriptwriting as a form of practical writing (see Chapter 1): The person who writes the script for the digital story is the same one who produces it. There are no separate actors, directors, or artists.

For these reasons, then, you might see (and choose to use) a script format that looks as pared-down and intuitive as the one in Figure 5.1.

Yet even in this simple form, certain key ideas are evident. The spoken text (which could just as easily be signified by the word *narration*) takes priority. Also, the section for images isn't merely a description of the image (as one might find in movie or comic book scripts) but contains a space to note the file name that corresponds to that image; this illustrates the supremely practical aspect of such a script, as does the aforementioned emphasis on assembling or compiling a narrative out of preexisting media products.

Figure 5.1. Sample Digital Story Script Template (A)

1. Spoken: _____ _____ Image File: _____ Image: _____
2. Spoken: _____ _____ Image File: _____ Image: _____
3. Spoken: _____ _____ Image File: _____ Image: _____
4. Spoken: _____ _____ Image File: _____ Image: _____
5. Spoken: _____ _____ Image File: _____ Image: _____

Figure 5.2 is an example of a slightly more sophisticated script format for digital stories. Note that the narration section includes the possibility of more than one audio file, a situation you'll encounter if music or sound effects are desired in between phrases of narration or playing under it, as an accompaniment. More important, note how the visual is broken out from auditory. Implicit here is the idea that the visual can be changed, either in theory or in practice (with a different file), so that it better supports the narration. The two are not considered an indivisible unit, but as discrete media elements that can be played with during the revision stage of writing (or even later).

So here's the interesting part—notice how similar this is to the two-column script format for videos as presented in the Making Friends with the Format section. This is not just another reason why these two media are both presented in this chapter—it shows that you can actually *teach* both at the same time. With this in mind, and only if you're comfortable because it fits your needs, you can provide a template like the one in Figure 5.3, in which "Image" and "Video" are conflated. That way a single script format can be used for either video or digital stories.

What are the advantages of this template? Well, you may have noticed that there are no write-on lines within the image/video cell. That's because students can draw (or print, cut, and paste) visuals directly into the space provided since the cells are deep enough (and the file names are written elsewhere) to accommodate a decent-sized picture when the template is used at its full size. In this way, storyboarding and scripting really become one process. Alternately—and this can really help sharpen descriptive writing skills—you can add lines to that

Figure 5.2. Sample Digital Story Script Template (B)

Narration (or other audio)	Image
1. _____ _____ (files: _____)	1. (files: _____)
2. _____ _____ (files: _____)	2. (files: _____)
3. _____ _____ (files: _____)	3. (files: _____)
4. _____ _____ (files: _____)	4. (files: _____)
5. _____ _____ (files: _____)	5. (files: _____)

Figure 5.3. Sample Digital Story Script Template (C)

Image/Video	File(s)	Audio/Narration	File(s)
1.			
2.			
3.			
4.			
5.			

image cell and have students compose "text storyboards," which are brief passages that supply details about the kind of image that will work for that segment of narration or audio.

The bottom line is that you will want to experiment a bit, adapting the script format for the project at hand to the kind of students you're working with, and to the type of software tools you're using (some may even have built-in script templates).

SKILLS FOCUS: RESPONSE TO LITERATURE

On the first page of the Introduction I suggested that print, which in English curricula usually means literature, is not incompatible with newer forms of media. Well, here's a tangible example of that principle: You can use scriptwriting as a way to deepen engagement with literature, whether popular or canonical or somewhere in between, by having students respond to those conventional print texts in ways that are unconventional. And that element of newness can spark not just the motivation to write, but also deeper and more personal ways of engaging with, and thinking about, the texts that we always hoped would inspire students.

Book Trailers

Video poetry based upon work written by others is a more than valid form of having students respond to literature. So is scripting a digital book trailer, an increasingly popular multimedia writing product that can be done for titles read in class or as part of independent reading. To be clear, book trailers are not intended to replace book reports, critical essays, reading journals, and other methods of writing about literature. They do, however, provide a great way to combine elements of these methods with persuasive writing and to make students engage with texts in new ways.

Like movie trailers, book trailers function both as previews (i.e., partial summaries) and sales pitches. Conduct a close reading with students of dust jacket or catalog copy so that they can develop a sense of the language of sales and marketing as it relates to books. As students script digital book trailers, they will want to be aware of these key elements of, and guidelines for, trailers in general:

1. Consider the audience first.
2. Draw the viewer in with an image, idea, or moment.
3. Summarize the story and quickly profile the main characters without giving too much away.
4. Mention the title and creator (in this case, the author) once the viewer is already hooked.
5. Keep things brief. Trailers that last more than a minute or 2 may start to feel sluggish, dissipating their own energy by overstaying their welcome.
6. Search the text for compelling quotes to use—a trailer should preview the content itself, not just be a summary of it.
7. Choose words with punch. Keep the tone enthusiastic and the voice colloquial.
8. Establish the dramatic tension or central problem. Leave viewers wanting to know what happens.
9. Cite anything else that is noteworthy in or about the book.
10. Provide the title for the audience at least once more before the ending. Build credibility by citing other works by the author, awards the book has won, or positive reviews it has received.
11. Also let the audience know about any other pertinent information for follow-up, such as the URL of the book's official website, its publication date (or paperback publication date), or where it is available for purchase or loan.

Finally, consider providing sentence-starters like the following:

- In a world where . . .
- It's a very bad day for [character name] . . .
- Meet [character name] . . .
- [Author name] has done it again . . .

Or you can view movie, book, and video game trailers with students and jot down other frequently occurring tropes—it's okay if students want to satirize trailers generally even as they create their own. An additional benefit of satire is that it requires students to engage in high-level thinking skills that depend on critical analysis.

Digital Scene Adaptations

Like scripting video poetry, adapting other forms of literature to digital multimedia provides a powerful way to connect reading and writing. Again, keep in mind that students *can* script a portion of text as video to be acted out much in the manner of a short film. This video can then stand on its own or be incorporated into a digital production that features graphics, such as a book cover and illustrations.

But before students dive creatively into ideas about how to embellish a scene from a novel or short story by adding animation, sound effects, original artwork, and so on, encourage them to return to the text. Explain that an effective adaptation of any literary work attempts to do justice to the original work within the parameters of the new medium, not simply serve as a point of departure for scriptwriters to indulge in their own original ideas. Here are some suggestions to help guide students' reexamination of a text with an eye to appropriating part of it for a script.

1. Start with a vital practical consideration: How long do you want the scene to be? A minute will probably feel too skimpy, but if the intention is actually to produce the script at a later date, a runtime of more than 5 minutes will typically entail a *lot* of production work. If a student is intent on adapting a 50-page battle scene that's the centerpiece of a novel, that's fine. Just help him or her apply the twin skills of abridgement and summary.
2. Think about which scenes are not only highly dramatic but also represent ones that an audience can appreciate without knowledge of the larger work.
3. Of these scenes, which provide video or audio "fodder" for a script, and preferably both? For example, passages that contain mostly internal thought processes or emotions are not going to be as easy to translate into visual terms. In contrast, text that speaks to the five

senses—especially hearing and sight—can present rich opportunities for adaptation.

4. Pay close attention to phrases and individual words. Which ones stand out for their impact or poetic power?
5. Of these words and phrases, which would best be suited to a visual? Similarly, which might serve as the basis for an audio element such as a sound effect?

Also, a caveat: For students adapting a scene from a popular work, *discourage* them from using stills or artwork from movie versions, such as *The Hunger Games* or *Harry Potter* franchises. Instead, stress that the goal of their scripts is to provide their *own* interpretations of these works. If students will be using non-original, copyrighted media, make sure that their scripts show how that media is used in a "transformative" way, thus allowing its inclusion under the principle of fair use. Examples of transforming media might be adding details to a piece of artwork, mixing two pieces of music together, or recording brand-new dialogue for an existing character. (For more on fair use, see Additional Resources, Appendix A.)

SKILLS FOCUS: PERSUASIVE WRITING

Whether students are writing a script for a PSA, commercial, or book trailer, they are engaged in persuasive writing. In their scripts, they may be tempted to include ideas and content that is fun to write or produce but that does not address their intended audience or further their intended purpose. Caution students about this aspect of writing for media—the constantly occurring opportunities for creativity can cause writers to include information and embellishments that are unnecessary.

In some types of scripts this tendency might be more acceptable but not in persuasive writing, which should omit irrelevant information and stay on track by supporting its main argument with details, examples, and sources that are ordered clearly and logically.

However, if students have studied propaganda and the biased presentations of facts in persuasive texts, it's worth reminding them to avoid these traits in their own scripts. In particular, you'll want to caution them to stay away from the following:

- *Bandwagon appeals.* It's fine for a script to depict a group of enthusiastic people engaged in a behavior or activity that it's advocating—this helps portray things in a positive light. But scripts should avoid a peer-pressure approach, where the underlying message of the visuals or the audio is, "Everyone's doing *x*, so you should, too."
- *Loaded language and other incidents of semantic bias.* While they're revising their scripts, encourage students to check each word they use not only

for its denotation but for its connotation as well. In addition, caution them against hyperbole and misleading exaggeration despite the prevalence of real-world examples in the advertising they see every day. (However, exaggerated language and images can be acceptable when clearly presented in a tongue-in-cheek manner for humorous effect.)

- *Misleading visuals.* Ask students if they've seen those TV commercials that, in trying to pitch a convenience device or time-saver, feature an actor struggling to perform some simple task and failing spectacularly (e.g., using a can opener and somehow managing to injure himself and ruin dinner at the same time). Explain that this is not the kind of script you expect from them—unless such absurdity is intentional and part of a parody.

SKILLS FOCUS: RESEARCH

Students who have not previously embraced research can find themselves motivated when the research serves as the backbone of a video or digital story. Certainly video is a great medium for documentaries and news spots since editing diverse source footage is relatively easy with the technology tools available today. Plus, direct experience with editing the "news" and related nonfiction products, and thereby learning how the presentation of facts to an audience is highly selective, is a great way for students to pick up media literacy skills while ostensibly working on an English assignment.

However, point out to students that they need to make a paper edit of the factual information in their scripts while they're developing them, and well before any actual editing of video segments or footage (for more on paper edits, see Ideas for Revising in this chapter). To support the use of reliable, accurate, and impactful sources, bring the following points to students' attention:

1. Research for expository or informational scripts involves two different, but related, processes. The first is researching relevant facts through methods that students are familiar with, including recording firsthand experience, conducting web searches, exploring reference resources, and so on. The second process involves researching the media artifacts—photographs, sound bites, archival footage—that the script will feature. Clarify that in many instances the research methods for media are identical to those for facts; however, they are sometimes complicated by the additional responsibility of securing permission for each piece of media to make sure it's okay to use.

2. Guide students to evaluate critically any sources of images and media the same way that they would vet other sources of information. This is especially true when it comes to that rich repository of downloadable media known as the Internet. Some curricula state that sources from

educational (.edu sites) and government institutions (.gov) should be trusted in almost all cases, but you'll want to remind students to follow whatever guidelines are in effect in your school.

3. Remind students that script drafts can spec an audio or video element in a general way rather than citing an actual image or file. They can then use the script as the basis to conduct research and *then* revise the script according to the audio or visual resources that they find.

4. The combining of two "modalities" like this can be powerful–but scriptwriters need to take care that they're not creating fallacious associations with, say, the audio discussing one event and the video depicting another that resembles it. To avoid misleading the audience, scriptwriters can specify video that's obviously generic or use on-screen text to subtly point out the incongruity between image and word.

5. Scriptwriters should consider converting facts and statistics into visuals whenever they might clarify complex data or make a point more forcefully. Students should also know that many software applications include handy tools for translating data into pie charts, bar graphs, and other visual aids.

6. Scripts should cite the source of figures and statistics either in the audio track or via on-screen text. If a "talking head" is giving an opinion in a video, an on-screen identifier (much like a caption) can provide the person's name, academic institution, or other information. Viewers can't flip to the bibliography or endnotes to check on a source in a video as they can when reading a research report or other print texts, which is why as many sources as possible should be cited at point-of-use.

7. Finally, research doesn't just mean library or computer work; it may entail interviewing people (see the prewriting section that follows) or other ways of collecting evidence and information firsthand–creating primary source material rather than simply using existing primary sources.

LITERACY ACROSS THE DISCIPLINES: DOCUMENTARIES THAT "SHOW WHILE YOU TELL"

Because documentaries have become an increasing popular genre in recent years, you may have wondered why they were not covered in Chapter 4. By now, though, the reason should be clear: Quite often scripting and producing documentaries involves repurposing existing footage or recording new footage that is decidedly unscripted, which pretty much sums up video and digital storytelling as presented here.

Unlike fiction scripts (Chapter 4's topic), documentary scripts match informational and/or persuasive text to complementary visuals. For social studies, a teacher might assign student teams to produce a biographical segment or re-create a historical event with added analysis (to prevent it from being historical fiction), or to report on the characteristics or practices of a particular society, culture, or subculture. (See "Adapting Oral Histories" in Chapter 6 for a related possibility.) For science, students might be asked to script a video or digital documentary about a specific biological system or to warn about environmental dangers.

In all of these instances the approach should be the same. First, students would benefit from revisiting, or just visiting, the previous Skills Focus section on research. Any documentarian will tell you that research is the foundation of any project. While drafting, students should create a cohesive presentation by adding a unifying device such as a voice-over, as in any video or digital storytelling script format. This documentary can be developed as an alternative to a research paper on a topic in the disciplines or as an offshoot of one, repurposing all the research (including any original experimentation or ethnography) already done for a paper but for a new medium and, one would hope, wider audience.

THE WRITING PROCESS

Ideas for Prewriting

Prewriting is arguably more crucial to video and digital storytelling scripts than other kind of scripts—one might even legitimately claim that scriptwriting in these cases consists *mostly* of prewriting. That is, the gathering of information and media resources and the planning of the order of their presentation is the most important part of the process, with the finished script even looking somewhat like a graphic organizer.

Still, students should recall that the first drafts of video scripts can specify that original footage be shot, original graphics created, and so on. You can have students stop after this point if you don't intend for them to produce a finished product because, in essence, they've written a script. *If* actual video will be shot or *if* assets will be collected or created for a multimedia presentation, then they can also view that draft as a precursor, so it's still part of the prewriting process. Then they will begin their real drafting once the pieces are available and can be slotted into the script with confidence.

One question students are likely to have regarding a digital story is, "How long should it be?" Their academic level and the purpose of the digital story will, of course, inform how you answer this question. As a rule, consider that most images will be held on screen for about 10 to 15 seconds, which for ten images works out to a maximum of 150 seconds, or 2.5 minutes. A persuasive piece, however, may present a quick succession of facts and statistics to build its argument; as a result, images will be on screen for between 5 and 10 seconds. On the other hand, a first-person narrative, the most common form of digital story, should contain plenty of absorbing details in the spoken part of the script; consequently, listeners may be captivated by the voice telling them the story and not care so much about how quickly the images change, allowing 20 seconds or more for each.

Keep in mind that gathering the media necessary for a script need not be terribly involved. As mentioned earlier, students can simply take pictures with any handy camera (or even a mobile phone) or use clip art that's available for free use. They might be able to shoot brief video segments with a regular digital camera as well.

For persuasive or expository (e.g., documentary-style) digital stories, students may want to include infographics as needed. That's fine, but advise them to keep these simple in design and message because they can't assume that their audience will have the time or screen size to take in anything too detailed. Like other graphics used to provide facts, an infographic should be clear and bold.

When selecting a topic for a script, either as a class or working with individual students, consider the adaptation of traditional writing projects into production scripts. This can be not only a strong motivator for students to complete more traditional writing assignments but also a way for them to hit the ground running with their scriptwriting since they already have the raw material that typically needs to be gathered or planned during the prewriting stage. In addition, writing adaptations will present a wealth of opportunities to talk through both the strengths and limitations of writing prose versus writing for audio and visual languages, and to reflect on the elements of that traditional writing product through a new lens.

Encourage visual learners and other students to use the storyboard process (see Chapter 4) to plan their video and digital storytelling scripts.

Conducting Interviews

A frequent key component of news spots and other informational scripts is a prerecorded interview. Students should conduct and transcribe interviews in the prewriting stage so they can then have a full visual/audio text to break up and use as needed throughout their scripts. And of course conducting interviews is an excellent opportunity to develop speaking and listening skills. Here are some ideas for making the interview process smoother for your students:

- They can write their questions well in advance and then rehearse them with a partner, making sure that both the questions' meaning and their delivery are clear. These mock interviews can not only provide self-confidence but can also help refine the wording of the questions.
- Emphasize the importance of open-ended questions that begin with words such as *How* or *Why*. These will elicit longer, more interesting responses.
- Let students know that it's okay to repeat a question during taping or to request that an answer be repeated. This might be necessary because of poor enunciation or volume or of word choice that can be improved upon.

- Point out that the asking of the questions can be eliminated in the editing process so that only the answer appears on the video. This should help if students are self-conscious about their own appearance or voice.
- For sit-down interviews, coach students to ask their subjects to try to paraphrase the question itself as part of their answer—that way, during production, the interviewer's voice can be cut from the audio altogether, leaving a stronger stand-alone sound bite that can be used for a variety of purposes, such as voice-over.
- Students shouldn't forget that interviews can be used in digital stories as well. That doesn't mean that they would be placed on the audio track as a replacement for narration but rather that a revealing (but relatively brief) quote could appear on the screen for the audience to read.

Ideas for Drafting

For students scripting digital stories there is probably one writing element above all others that they should take special care with during the drafting stage: *voice*. A common (and commonsense) precept holds that when the script text is eventually narrated it should not *feel* as if it's being read—after all, the medium is called digital *storytelling*, not "digital scriptreading." What I'd like to point out, however, is that this is not an issue that one needs to wait to address until the rehearsal stage, as some digital storytelling experts may imply. Yes, simply trying to deliver the narration text with a conversational-sounding voice *is* desired. Still, why not ensure success by planting the seeds for this back at the drafting stage? Advise students to eschew fancy words (such as *eschew*) and instead focus on the authenticity that comes from personal beliefs, feelings, and experiences (or any combination thereof).

Students should bear in mind the elastic definition of drafting when it comes to drafting video scripts that are not prescriptive in the sense of radio dramas or TV sitcoms. The writing process becomes potentially more recursive each time a piece of media or a segment of video is spec'd—some material won't be located or created, and other material that has been gathered may not work for reasons of quality, lack of permission to use it, or incompatible technology. That means the writer will have to tweak the script. As a result, the line between drafting and revising can become blurred over successive iterations of the script: Revisions can take place almost on the heels of prewriting, and entire new passages may need to be drafted fairly late in the process.

Students should keep in mind that even digital stories that contain only static images (such as photos or illustrations) can have "movement." This movement is not just in the form of transitions, wherein one image can slide out of the way to reveal a new one, but it also applies to movement within a single image: Pans, **zooms**, and reverse zooms are fairly common. Advise students to use such devices in ways that are appropriate to the narrative or informational purpose. For example, use a zoom when the scripted narration itself moves from general to specific or a reverse zoom when the intention is to focus on an item and then reveal a surprising context or background for it. In fact, when there is no storytelling purpose like these, then transitions should not even appear in the script but rather be left to the production phase when they can be made for purely aesthetic reasons.

Have students recall the concept of "See Dog, Say Dog" and ask themselves whether they are underusing or overusing it as they draft. Again, it can either be a powerful device or come across as simpleminded, depending on the context.

As a follow-up to the preceding tip, caution students that "See Dog, Say Dog" especially applies to when on-screen print is presented for reading. That's because both videos and digital stories don't work if they force viewers to process two *different* texts from language-based media, voice-over and print text, simultaneously. One is sure to be shortchanged in terms of attention when the brain attempts this kind of multitasking.

How detailed should music specs be in the first draft of a video or digital story script? Explain to students that there's something to be said for keeping the reference as generic as possible, indicating its genre, mood, and perhaps instrumentation but nothing more; specific tracks that fit these parameters can then be identified during the production process. However, music can completely change the message sent by its corresponding image, and thus affect the tone of the digital story or video overall; leaving things too generic (e.g., "some classical music"), then, can lead to problems down the road. So as contradictory as it may sound, you'll want to coach students to be as precise as possible about the particular mood or tone they want the music to evoke, but as open-ended as possible in terms of the actual piece of music that fulfills the script's needs in these respects.

Remind students to add production credits at the end of their scripts or at least placeholder text for the credits. Typically, credits scroll on the screen, but they can also be presented by photographing handwritten or typed signs.

Differentiated Instruction

Below-Level Students Can . . .

- Draft digital stories in prose with paragraph breaks and skipped lines to create "chunks" of text. In fact, teachers sometimes have on-level students do this, first revising this nonscript format before any media is spec'd for it.
- Begin crafting digital stories by simply drawing storyboard-like images outside of any script format, then verbally rehearse and tell a story that connects the images rather than trying to draft a script per se. After they can comfortably and effectively narrate their stories, they can record their own voices and transcribe what they have said, removing any asides, errors, awkward phrases, and the like. This transcription can then serve as the basis for a formal script.

- Repurpose monologues (from Chapter 1) or any first-person narratives they've written for use as the backbone of a digital story; their familiarity with the content should help them focus on scripting the additional media elements.
- Partner with students whose skills complement theirs. Scripting, let alone producing, video and multimedia projects can be challenging for any student. The more a division of labor exists—between, say, researching, spec'ing or creating media, and organizing the flow of a script—the less chance there is of below-level students becoming overwhelmed.
- Summarize texts and events verbally before writing scripts based upon them. That way you can ensure comprehension or recall during the prewriting stage.
- Leverage their prior knowledge by scripting on-air promos for shows that they're fans of or scripting book trailers for their favorite books.
- Cut back on the duration of their scripts. PSAs, for example, can be as brief as 15 seconds—as little as half a page of script, depending on how it's formatted and how much visual detail is included.

English Language Learners Can . . .

- Translate scripts written in their native language into English via subtitles—or vice versa.
- Benefit from extra rehearsal time if they'll be delivering a voice-over. Assure them of this so they don't shy away from including oral roles for themselves in their scripts. Alternately, they can employ on-screen text in place of a voice-over, provided that the audience doesn't feel that it's simply reading an entire video or presentation.
- Use storyboards to order the elements in their scripts and get your feedback on the organization before putting their ideas into words.
- Learn from you and other students any culturally based forms of media they might not be familiar with, such as PSAs. Terminology can become clearer after you explain the relevant word origins; for example, "trailers" used to trail, or follow, movies in theaters, not precede them, and "promo" is short for "promotion."

Advanced Students Can . . .

- Choose to script an infomercial, which combines elements of a commercial but in a form closer to the length of a TV episode. The topic need not be consumer goods but instead can center on a charitable cause or a public policy issue, thus making the media product more closely resemble an extended PSA than a commercial.
- Repurpose, either in part or in total, media they have created elsewhere (e.g., a podcast or a digital comic) in their digital story scripts.
- Research in advance any opportunities to publish their finished projects electronically, such as on your town's website or on a nonprofit's YouTube channel. They would then have to consider the limitations and content guidelines of such outlets when writing their scripts.

Ideas for Revising

Frequent rehearsals should be part of the revising process and should really even begin during the drafting stage. That is, writers must constantly monitor their work for brevity and expressiveness, both in digital stories and videos. Can the text for any given image be read or narrated within the intended time frame?

Students should conduct paper edits with the eye of a producer. Is everything in the script really feasible in terms of time, budget, or availability? If not, changes should be made.

Students should also double-check that audio and video work well together at every point in their two-column scripts. You might want to encourage them to create thumbnail sketches of the visuals on index cards and have someone read the audio portion aloud as they flip from one image to the next.

During the revision stage, scriptwriters should analyze whether certain words are being repeated in ways that are not obvious. For example, a sound bite, the narration, and some text graphics might all feature the same word in the course of a minute. This fact might not leap out from a casual reading of the script but will surely be evident to the audience. Scriptwriters need to master the art of altering their own word choices as often as necessary since it's less feasible to replace words where they are spoken or written in existing media.

Point out that viewers will remember the first and last things said or presented in a video. This is a concept that scriptwriters can use to their advantage in persuasive pieces, but it's also one that they must take care in exercising lest they emphasize the wrong things.

Reproduce and distribute the Digital Storytelling and Video Revision Checklist in Appendix B. Advise students to refer to these as they strengthen their scripts through revision. You can also share the Digital Storytelling and Video rubric in Appendix C.

WRAP-UP

Multimodal communication surrounds students—all of us, really—in ways that are so ubiquitous that they are in danger of going unnoticed. That web banner or that highway billboard one passes at 60 miles per hour—the one that contains a simple image of a burger or pizza, a restaurant name, and an exit number—these media products, ephemeral as they may seem, rely on our ability to process multiple streams of information.

By explicitly "teasing apart" the distinct text tracks provided in multimodal products, students not only learn the characteristics of different ways of communicating, but enhance their media literacy skills as well. Of course the end result is actually heightened critical literacy, as, having learned techniques "from the inside out," they can now grasp how various texts position them by their combination of media and by how scriptwriters have allocated certain strands of information to a specific medium.

CHAPTER 6

FURTHER ADVENTURES IN SCRIPTWRITING

The purpose of this chapter is to present a few ideas that don't fit so neatly into the previous chapters but in many cases represent the most engaging and challenging scriptwriting projects you could tackle with your students. Once they've come to realize the truth, not just intellectually but through experience, of the notion stated in the Introduction—that scriptwriting forms the basis of most of the narrative and informational media they enjoy—they'll want to start applying their newfound skills in all sorts of novel ways.

That means they may even want to combine elements from different kinds of scripts and, in the process, could even come up with new forms of media. In that sense, the scripts that follow are intended as a modest form of inspiration. Of course all of these scripts support the writing curriculum in some way, but because there is so much ground to cover, we'll dispense with some of the typical features in previous chapters such as detailed notes on the writing process. I hope that's okay with you since you're an old hand at teaching scriptwriting by now.

WHY TEACH THIS?

In addition to the reasons mentioned above and all the curricular connections that will occur to you, the miscellaneous scripts covered in the pages that follow have other uses as well: independent portfolio projects, cross-disciplinary work, enrichment or extension activities, schoolwide events and performances (e.g., assemblies), and so on. They should also suggest various rewarding ways to collaborate with colleagues who are arts or media teachers or edtech specialists.

Common Core State Standards for Skills Focus

L.7.4. Determine or clarify the meaning of unknown and multiple-meaning words and phrases based on grade 7 reading and content, choosing flexibly from a range of strategies.

W.7.2a. Introduce a topic clearly, previewing what is to follow; organize ideas, concepts, and information, using strategies such as definition, classification, comparison/contrast, and cause/effect; include formatting (e.g., headings), graphics (e.g., charts, tables), and multimedia when useful to aiding comprehension.

W.7.2c. Use appropriate transitions to create cohesion and clarify the relationships among ideas and concepts.

SL.7.4. Present claims and findings, emphasizing salient points in a focused, coherent manner with pertinent descriptions, facts, details, and examples; use appropriate eye contact, adequate volume, and clear pronunciation.

SL.7.6. Adapt speech to a variety of contexts and tasks, demonstrating command of formal English when indicated or appropriate.

L.11–12.4. Determine or clarify the meaning of unknown and multiple-meaning words and phrases based on grades 11–12 reading and content, choosing flexibly from a range of strategies.

W.11–12.2a. Introduce a topic; organize complex ideas, concepts, and information so that each new element builds on that which precedes it to create a unified whole; include formatting (e.g., headings), graphics (e.g., figures, tables), and multimedia when useful to aiding comprehension.

W.11–12.2c. Use appropriate and varied transitions and syntax to link the major sections of the text, create cohesion, and clarify the relationships among complex ideas and concepts.

SL.11–12.4. Present information, findings, and supporting evidence, conveying a clear and distinct perspective, such that listeners can follow the line of reasoning, alternative or opposing perspectives are addressed, and the organization, development, substance, and style are appropriate to purpose, audience, and a range of formal and informal tasks.

SL.11–12.6. Adapt speech to a variety of contexts and tasks, demonstrating a command of formal English when indicated or appropriate. (NGA Center & CCSSO, 2010, pp. 42–46)

Skills Preview

In this chapter, you will learn to help students do the following:

- Write scripts for a range of media forms not typically associated with scripts: live multimedia events, picture books, social media, and reality TV
- Express themselves creatively with script types such as those for transmedia and video games
- Adapt oral histories into a variety of other media
- Hone their persuasive writing skills by scripting promos in one medium for a media product in a *different* medium
- Synthesize and reflect upon what they have learned about scriptwriting—and writing generally—as a result of composing for media

MULTIMEDIA EVENTS

Multimedia, while hardly a new term, continues to be reinvented with new media and new technology (as we saw in the previous chapter). Yet ultimately multimedia need not be technology driven at all. A couple of students acting out a scene while another displays a placard with text for the audience to read and a fourth plays music—either live or recorded—is without question a multimedia experience.

A successful multimedia event, then, can combine elements of theatrical performance and audiovisual presentations to create a dazzling exercise in public speaking. To create such events, have students revisit the basic ideas involved in creating a video or digital story script presented in Chapter 5, such as making sure that the specific media *type* and *content* support the delivery of the underlying message in a way that's aligned with both audience and purpose. Instead of scripting the presentation in a two-column format, tell students to use the format for stage plays—or encourage them to invent a hybrid of the two formats.

Multimedia events usually kick off gatherings such as all-company meetings, press conferences, and the like. Students can create such events for assemblies and other special occasions, such as commencement. This can be a project for an entire class or a group of committed students, and it can be done entirely within the English language arts classroom or in cooperation with faculty in the arts, media, and technology departments.

PICTURE BOOKS

Scripting picture books is a writing project that's perfect as a precursor or follow-up to scripting comics or as an alternative at lower grade levels or in a remedial context. Students can work in pairs or trios so that each gets a chance to script a story as well as serve on the art team that illustrates it. They can rotate through these positions on the same text or over the course of scripting and illustrating different books. Simply make a copy of the easy-to-use template provided in Figure 6.1.

To keep the project manageable, model the process and, if time permits, in a whole-class or small-group configuration produce one or two pages of script and the corresponding art for it. This can help you set appropriate parameters for a given grade level or group of students, determining how much text should be on a page, how long it takes to create art at a certain level of detail, and so on. This in turn can help you decide the page range for the finished script or book, how much time the assignment should take, and other important factors.

Figure 6.1. Sample Picture Book Script Template

Title/Author: _____

Page Number: _____

Description of Art: _____

Sketch/Thumbnail of Art (optional):

```
┌──────────────────────────────────────────────────────────┐
│                                                            │
│                                                            │
│                                                            │
│                                                            │
│                                                            │
│                                                            │
│                                                            │
│                                                            │
└──────────────────────────────────────────────────────────┘
```

Text: _____

_____

_____

_____

_____

CROSS-MEDIA PROMOS

Remember the discussion of on-air promos (Chapter 5's QuickStart)? A variation on that idea involves scripting a cross-media promo, which means a promo in one medium for a work that appears in another. For instance, a podcast can draw attention to a student-created mini-comic or to a digital story that's now available on your school's website—or vice versa.

Does your school have daily announcements over the public address system? See if your students can script a brief text for that audio broadcast to promote an upcoming school play or issue of the literary magazine. They'll get a chance to use their persuasive writing skills and perhaps incorporate sound effects and music—even a live performance like this can be perked up by having students push a button to play recorded audio of this sort. The goal here isn't just engagement; it's to provide a real-world context and purpose for student scriptwriting, thereby making it more authentic.

TRANSMEDIA STORYTELLING

Perhaps the most exciting way you could have students both extend and demonstrate what they have learned about scripts in general is to have them create a transmedia project.

How is transmedia different from "cross-media"? Well, the former isn't simply an adaptation from one medium to another. Instead, transmedia attempts to "immerse" audiences in its storyworld by distributing its narrative over multiple platforms by design. In short, there's no way to follow, let alone appreciate, the story from just a single medium.

The writing task, then, is quite simple—yet hardly easy.

Students need to write scripts for whatever media they would like to employ to tell their tales, and decide in what order (if any) the narrative should unfold. That's the simple part: There's no real requirement to write a "transmedia script"—it's really just all the other script forms students already know. The tricky part comes in all the planning. Remember the idea of a series "bible," first discussed back in Chapter 4? With transmedia properties that bible becomes even more important as it helps determine which aspects of the overarching story are told via different media or platforms.

ADAPTING ORAL HISTORIES

Having students elicit, record, and transcribe oral histories is a common project in English language arts curricula. But rather than transcribing an oral history into standard prose paragraphs, why not have students adapt it into a script? There are several possibilities here, including the following:

1. The oral history can provide the backbone for a podcast or a series of podcasts (depending on the length of the text). Students can script host intros, sound effects, and music that supports and matches the content of the text.

2. Students can script a short film that dramatizes an incident that the oral history recounts. The recording of the oral history can function as the soundtrack, with performers acting out its details without actually saying dialogue.

3. A video script can help students create a compelling biographical profile. The oral history can be one of the audio sources in the right-hand column—so, too, can a narrator who paraphrases passages from it and supplies historical context as necessary.

4. Most obviously, because this is a common premise for the medium's content, a digital storytelling script can provide images and sounds that depict the historical period of the oral history. The emphasis on

voice in both senses of the word—an actual voice and one's "voice" as a writer or narrator of events—makes digital stories perhaps the perfect vehicle for oral histories of a certain length.

REALITY TV

As educators, we may dislike the vapidity of much of reality TV, but you can use the genre as an engaging tool to teach reportage, textual assemblage, and nonfiction narrative skills. Work with students and colleagues to enable the former to "shadow" one or more faculty members over a specified period of time.

The writing product can then be a video script that presents a "Day in the Life" of an engaging subject such as a phys ed teacher or band leader. To this end, students should work in groups of three to five to coordinate their individual schedules to create a master "shooting schedule" so they can capture the subject at different times—after all, it's not feasible for, say, a lone middle schooler to handle a task of this scale. Then, when all the footage is shot, the group can similarly divvy up the writing chores so that one student scripts supplemental interview questions, another the transitions, another the introduction or the wrap-up, and so on, so they can all contribute meaningfully to the script. In fact, that's a lot of writing for a television genre that's supposedly "unscripted"!

VIDEO GAME "CUT SCENES"

Video games do have scriptwriters, sometimes called "story designers" and the like, but they do not have the creative role that scriptwriters in other media do. Determining all the pathways along which a game can be played, as well as the entire "look and feel" of its world, is the job of a lead or senior game designer. This person manages a team of artists and programmers to create a comprehensive "design document" that may contain several scripted elements.

One of these is something called a **cut scene**. Although the gamers in your class will be well aware of this term, you just need to know that it refers to a brief, stand-alone segment that automatically plays between levels or at other key moments that bridge parts of the game or its narrative (i.e., it appears when the game **cuts** from one setting or task to another). The important thing is, because a cut scene is not part of the gameplay itself, it can be written in the format of a film or TV script. And that means that revisiting the skills and strategies discussed in Chapter 4 might be in order.

Other contributions that a nondesigner might make to a game could include writing dialogue or fleshing out a backstory for the characters, but these elements do not really shape the overall experience of the game that much. So although writing is certainly a critical skill to have in creating games, it's not scriptwriting per se. (Adding to the confusion is that "scripting" in video games actually refers to writing software code.) That said, students interested in writing games will find solid preparation for it in the other script formats in this book.

AUDIO COMMENTARIES

Audio commentaries on DVDs often sound like free-flowing conversations but often they are subtly scripted—the moderator may have an agenda to cover, and the group of commentators may have been instructed to touch upon certain topics. You can push this conceit a bit further by having students fully script a critical response to a recorded performance. The final product, an audio file of the script being performed, can be added as an alternate audio track to the original production if it's a student-created work, or it can just stand on its own as a file that viewers can play manually in sync with the film or TV show. Here are some points to keep in mind when considering this fun project:

- It should capitalize on students' prior familiarity with a given piece of moving-image media—commentary should not be based upon a first-time viewing. Instead, students should view the media product in advance and take notes on it.
- You can position this activity as a form of responding to literature by having students record a commentary to a movie version of a literary work—anything from Shakespeare to J. K. Rowling.
- Have students return to the original print text and take notes so that they can comment from a "fidelity studies" perspective if they wish. How faithful was the movie to the book?
- Students on the same panel of commentators (limited to no more than five) should collaborate on the script and include "time code" notations so that specific points can be covered at precise moments in the movie or TV show. (To find out when these moments occur, they should click "display" or "info" on a DVD remote control or simply observe the progress bar if they're watching online or via some form of digital media viewer.)
- Remind students not to script their commentary in a strict, word-for-word manner that they feel they must adhere to. Instead, the script should feature summaries of points they want to make and, possibly, transitions between topics for the moderator to use. The potential for improvisation should be strong and apparent.
- With this in mind, encourage students to respond to each other while recording the commentary track. This will make the activity one of listening, not just speaking. It will also give participants an opportunity to depart from their scripted remarks.

- The commentary can be evaluative or personal, or even feature jokey criticism à la *Mystery Science Theater 3000*, as long as it's appropriate to the assignment.

LITERACY ACROSS THE DISCIPLINES: SOCIAL MEDIA DIALOGUE

This chapter references many interdisciplinary projects, but this activity spotlights an application of scriptwriting skills to the content areas not commonly explored: composing dialogue for platforms such as Facebook, Twitter, and Instagram.

Basically this is an exercise in role-playing, and in fact owes much to the "Time-Travel Dialogues" project described in Chapter 2. Here students can assume the parts of historical figures or famous scientists engaged in a social media "conversation" via replies to each other's posts or comments. As preparation, students should conduct research, especially in terms of biographical material, to learn not just what leaders felt and thought but also things like the phrases they might have actually used in everyday exchanges.

Working singly or in pairs, students can script this dialogue and then transfer it online to accounts they set up for just this purpose. Remind them not to forget the equivalent of directions or parentheticals (see Chapter 4's script model), which online are often signaled with asterisks: *shrugs.*

So where does the element of performance enter the picture? Well, that's actually provided by the audience, which can fully interact with the dialogue by commenting on specific posts, rating them, and then of course replying to each other's comments and ratings.

TESOL SKILLS FOCUS: EXPRESSIVE VOCABULARY AND ORAL LANGUAGE

Like writing other texts, writing scripts can enhance expressive vocabulary, provided that students focus on things such as word choice, shades of meaning, and learning new content-area or academic terminology along the way. Scripts also add another dimension to vocabulary development since such a large portion of them involves speech in some form. To turn this potential into actual opportunities for all students, and English language learners in particular, to practice oral language, consider these suggestions:

- Ask students to read scripts aloud regardless of whether there are any plans to actually produce them. Have you ever seen a radio drama performed live? It's a unique and wonderful form of theater that you can use as a surrogate for audio recordings if these are not feasible to do. Similarly, you can use photocopies of a comic book script as the basis for Readers' Theatre—simply assign the role of narrator to one student who'll read all the descriptions of the artwork and any captions.

- Invite other classes and parents to a "table read" of a film, television, or video script. Point out that such informal, but highly expressive, readings of a script are a regular part of the show business world.
- Encourage oral improvisation in the above-mentioned performances. In fact, let students know that such directions can be built directly into their scripts with the addition of a single phrase: AD-LIB; for example: "The partygoers AD-LIB post-dinner chitchat while the band TUNES its instruments" or "Roger, now frantic, AD-LIBS orders to his crew to throw him a life jacket."
- Before having students ad-lib, work as a group to develop a menu of vivid verbs and precise nouns that is informed by the context of the script and that the students can draw upon while improvising. For instance, in the above example, ask students to decide whether Roger would actually use the word *throw* or whether *toss* or *fling* would be a better choice. (By the way, the answer is probably "yes" to the former and "no" to the latter.)

SKILLS FOCUS: SPATIAL, CHRONOLOGICAL, IMPORTANCE ORDER

Because they are so clearly organized, even to the point of calling out scene changes in sluglines, script formats are great for teaching sequence: Students can easily plan, and track, where they are presenting particular narrative or factual information. To teach patterns of text organization more explicitly, use the following strategies and ideas:

1. To reinforce spatial order, have students script an audio or video tour of a particular location—their neighborhood, their school, a historic landmark, or a wilderness area such as a state or a national park. Coach them to decide on a spatial organization based on factors, including an established route or pathway, cardinal directions, or elevation (highest to lowest points, or vice versa).
2. To reinforce chronological order, have students write both fiction and nonfiction scripts that clearly feature a "ticktock." That means adopting an explicitly time-driven method of structuring their ideas, such as including **intertitles** (text-only screens as in silent films) that call out the time or simply providing some kind of deadline, or both (think about the television show *24*). You also might want to challenge students to explore reverse chronology, the basis for episodes of *The X-Files* and *Star Trek: Voyager*. Normal or reverse chronology is very easy to signal with the narrative captions in comics, where calling attention to dates and times is less clunky than in other media.
3. To reinforce order of importance, have students focus on the many persuasive and expository projects that appear across media in this

book. In terms of the expository mode, encourage students to order information per news journalism's inverted pyramid, which is covered in Chapter 5.

4. Finally, consider establishing a unit where students can engage in scriptwriting across the curriculum. By partnering with a life sciences or social studies teacher, you can have students write scripts on topics, such as the water cycle or the civil rights movement, that intrinsically suggest an ordered structure.

BRINGING IT ALL HOME: WRITING AND THINKING ACROSS MEDIA AND SCRIPT FORMATS

If your students have worked through any of the previous chapters, they'll have started to build a repertoire of scriptwriting and media terms, many of which apply across formats. For example, certain types of visual shots (**bird's-eye** view, close-up) are equally important across film, video, and comics. And, as students have learned, techniques such as voice-over narration can serve a variety of purposes across media. To prompt both critical thinking and deepened reflection on the scriptwriting projects that students have undertaken, start a discussion with questions such as these:

*   What type of scriptwriting or media did you learn the most about? How has it changed your attitude toward that particular medium?
*   In what ways can scriptwriting make writing in basic modes such as descriptive, expository, and narrative more—or less—enjoyable than when addressing them in prose text? Why?
*   Compare and contrast how the same formal elements are used across different media. For example, how does using voice-over in a film or TV show differ from using it in a podcast or digital story, which depends on audio narration?
*   What have you learned about scriptwriting? What kind(s) of scripts would you be interested in writing again at some point?
*   How is writing scripts different from writing poetry or prose? How is it similar?

CONCLUDING REMARKS

Teachers often search for that magical yet elusive "engagement pill"—the one that prompts students to interact with content on a deep and critical level, supports them in making text-to-self connections, uses technology that mimics or at least acknowledges their outside-of-school literacy practices, and gives them the opportunity for self-expression.

After reading this book, I hope you've come to the conclusion that scriptwriting is an outside candidate for magic engagement pill status, at least in the English language arts curriculum. I'm not sure what other compositional strategy can do the following:

- Consistently make nonfiction creative for students
- Help students create digital media and multimedia projects
- Foster authentic collaborative work in the spirit of the "21st-century skills"
- Inspire cross-curricular learning in conjunction with the visual and performing arts
- Enable extension and enrichment projects that truly extend and enrich the existing curriculum

Perhaps because all that sounds so new and great, it's easy to lose sight of the fact that scripts have always had a place in the ELA classroom, from Reader's Theatre to *Julius Caesar* and *Raisin in the Sun*. In fact, as a middle school teacher some years ago, I had to cover both of those dramatic works in my curriculum. I dutifully set about helping students study the text of both plays in order to mount productions. With *Julius Caesar*, I was even ambitious enough to start shooting a video version performed at various locations around the campus—and this was, of course, after I had screened film versions of these plays, as countless other teachers have done before and since.

Yet in all this reading, performing, watching, and talking, there was no clear and authentic connection to the writing curriculum, and only later did I realize that scriptwriting was the connective tissue that had been missing. In a sense, then, this is the book that I wish I'd had back then. So thanks for reading it—and please find me online and tell me what you think . . .

LinkedIn: www.linkedin.com/in/petergutierrez
Twitter: @Peter_Gutierrez

ADDITIONAL RESOURCES

COPYRIGHT AND FAIR USE

Students may want to use found footage, preexisting photos or art, or copyrighted music in videos and digital projects, so you should be aware of the issues surrounding such usage rather than prohibiting it outright. Empower yourself by first realizing that policies in your school or institution, originally developed as helpful rules of thumb, may be antiquated or, more alarmingly, have taken on the cast of rigid law rather than practical internal guidelines. Here are two places to go to get accurate and up-to-date information.

Stanford Copyright & Fair Use Center: http://fairuse.stanford.edu

Perhaps the definitive web resource on copyright, Fair Use, public domain content, and related issues, this site provides a wealth of information both to the scholar and the neophyte. This includes an FAQ section, the actual texts of the pertinent legal rulings and documents, links to the Open Content Alliance, policy statements, and a host of agencies and organizations.

NCTE's Guideline on the Code of Best Practices in Fair Use for Media Literacy Education: http://www.ncte.org/positions/statements/fairusemedialiteracy

Although you might tend to see yourself exclusively as an English teacher, when you begin instruction in media-based writing, you also become a media literacy educator. In fact, a central part of media literacy pedagogy is having students create their own media products, a process in which scriptwriting plays a key part. What kind of images or audio clips can students research and then sample in their own work? This guideline, adopted by NCTE and other leading organizations in 2008, clarifies the issue. It also contains links to a variety of free resources that spell out the established best practices in making documentaries and videos as well as teaching media literacy. (You might also want to read *Copyright Clarity: How Fair Use Supports Digital Learning* by Renee Hobbs, jointly published by Corwin and NCTE in 2010.)

SOFTWARE AND DIGITAL TOOLS (INCLUDING FREE STUFF!)

Digital Storytelling and Multimedia

Digital stories, which are mostly constructed of still images accompanied by voice-over narration, are covered in Chapter 5. The University of Virginia makes available a free, user-friendly web-based tool that allows students to script, choose images, and record narration online. This site also has plenty of resources and management tools for teachers: http://www.digitalstoryteller.org. Another great resource in this respect, one that is full of links to helpful (and usually free) media sources is maintained by the Graduate School of Library and Information Science at the University of Illinois at http://course-web.lis.illinois.edu/~jevogel2/lis506/howto.html.

For a tried-and-true resource for multimedia projects, head to VoiceThread.com, which charges less than $100 annually for a classroom subscription (up to 100 student accounts). Also an online tool that can be accessed from any computer, VoiceThread allows students to collaborate in ways that are both easy and fun, with features for incorporating still images, video, and text documents into slideshow-style presentations. Students can even use doodles to comment on each other's work by drawing directly "on top of" visuals. Want to know more about VoiceThread from an organization that helps students script and produce projects in schools? Then check out The Media Spot and its free video tutorial: http://themediaspot.org/voicethreadcom_tutorials_info.

Software, Storyboards, and Scriptwriting Templates

If you want to create your own template for a script, you can use Microsoft Word. Work with hard tabs and preformatted items (e.g., all caps for speaker IDs) by creating a .dot file rather than a .doc or .docx file. There are plenty of online resources if you want to learn more about this, including Microsoft's own resources: http://office.microsoft.com.

Most scriptwriting software tends to be geared toward professionals and can be quite expensive. Websites and magazines that specialize in screenwriting, or those that publish movie and TV scripts, often feature ads, articles, and reviews about such software products. There is also a free, open-source alternative: http://celtx.com. Many professionals use the downloadable tools at this website to write moving-image scripts as well as comic book scripts, stage plays, and radio dramas. Functional across a variety of computer platforms, Celtx can also help with storyboarding and a range of other preproduction and production processes should your students decide to produce their scripts.

For professional storyboarding samples (and other previsualization resources) across a variety of media, including short films, TV, and video advertisements, please visit http://www.storyboards-east.com/storybrd.htm.

Audio and Podcasting

Because podcasting has really taken off in schools in recent years, there are many resources available for educators. Personally, I've found the information and links at the mobile-oriented education site LearninginHand.com to be very useful. Among other things, you'll find Tony Vincent's excellent, comprehensive, and *free* PDF booklet entitled "Podcasting for Teachers and Students" at http://learninginhand.com/podcasting-booklet.

A leading national expert in K–12 podcasting and audio more generally is Chris Shamburg, whose *Student-Powered Podcasting: Teaching for 21st-Century Literacy* (ISTE, 2010) is a rich resource that includes tutorials on different software packages. One of these is Audacity, an easy-to-use tool for recording, editing, and manipulating sounds, which is available as a free download at http://audacity.sourceforge.net. However, if you don't feel like purchasing a book, Dr. Shamburg's blog is a constant source of both curricular and technological ideas. A great example is the following post on the importance of sound effects to even very simple audio scripts, complete with links to free sources for sound effects and music: http://podcourse.blogspot.com/2007/04/audio-theater-1.html.

SCRIPTS FOR CLASSROOM USE

Many scripts of classic films can be found published in book form, but please note that these are often really just transcripts. That means that someone has viewed a movie and written its content in script form after the fact. For reading scripts and comparing them to the finished film or TV episode, as in Chapter 1, these are almost "too perfect," as there will be a very close correspondence.

To illustrate the writing process and to present scripts more authentically, you are better off using a draft of a script or a "shooting script." Sometimes these can be found on DVDs as an extra, or on a film's official website. One robust resource that I highly recommend is the SimplyScripts website (www.simplyscripts.com), which has both free downloads and links hosted by movie studios where PDFs of scripts are available.

Film and TV scripts, however, are just two types of scripts, and it's important for students to have access to professional models across media. Scribd.com (pronounced "skribbed") is kind of like a massive online library combined with a publishing company that provides free material—new texts are always being uploaded from the community for other visitors to use. Among the millions of documents available on this safe, easy-to-use, and open site are countless scripts in a variety of formats. Just search on items such as "PSA Script," "Two-Column Script," or "Comic Script" and you'll get results that include many professional models suitable for classroom use: http://www.scribd.com.

Radio Drama

Generic Radio Workshop is a treasure trove of transcripts of classic OTR ("old-time radio") broadcasts in all genres, from comedy to horror and literary adaptations. Better still, all of the transcripts are free: http://www.genericradio.com.

Movie and Television Scripts

In addition to being arguably the web's best source for popular and classic film and TV scripts, SimplyScripts.com also provides audio and even anime scripts. Of particular interest to teachers of English Language Learners, however, is its repository of non-English scripts.

Select scripts from popular British TV series such as *Sherlock* and *Doctor Who* can be downloaded from the BBC's website, which also contains encouragement and information for beginning scriptwriters: http://www.bbc.co.uk/writersroom/scripts/.

ORGANIZATIONS AND SUPPORT

Center for Digital Storytelling: http://www.storycenter.org/

These days there are many resources geared toward educators interested in digital storytelling. However, this nonprofit's website may warrant special attention from teachers and students as it presents real-world successes to demonstrate the power of authentic writing. Indeed, this statement from the Center's "What We Believe" section may help inspire reluctant student writers: "People who believe they are mundane, uninteresting, or unmemorable possess beneath this mask a vivid, complex, and rich body of stories just waiting to be told." (Center for Digital Storytelling, 2013).

Script Frenzy

Sadly, this organization's annual scriptwriting event is now defunct. However, you can still find a wide range of resources for writing screenplays and teleplays at www.scriptfrenzy.org. Of particular value might be the educator-friendly archives that remain available via the page for its Young Writers Program (http://ywp.scriptfrenzy.org). The Young Writers Program had a mission of supporting students to write "screenplays, stage plays, TV shows, short films, comic book scripts, radio scripts" and other script formats.

A Note About Contests

There are numerous script contests out there for a variety of media, and these change from year to year. Many of these are supported by reputable organizations, such as film festivals that sponsor screenplay competitions in youth divisions, but beware of contests that are not run by nonprofits or established publishers; as with other forms of writing, there are some groups that exist solely to collect "entry fees" and therefore exploit aspiring writers. Also, keep in mind that many legitimate contests are geared toward teen writers, so middle schoolers may find themselves in competition with high schoolers.

Writers Guild of America

Although the Writer Guild of America's most valuable benefits are reserved for its members who write professionally for film, TV, radio, and news, don't forget to pay a visit to the organization's websites for highly authoritative links related to all facets of scriptwriting. At the WGA West site (http://www.wga.org) click on "Writing Tools," and at the WGA East site (http://www.wgaeast.org), click on "Resources" and then "Writing Tools."

REVISION CHECKLISTS

Scriptwriting Revision Checklist—General Application

Name: _____

Date: _____

If you are writing . . .	Did you make sure to . . .	✓
a script for any medium	• address the expectations of both the primary and secondary audiences?	
	• use formal elements (e.g., kinds of shots, sound effects, word balloons) in ways that convey information effectively and not just for their own sake?	
	• follow any and all writing guidelines that apply from analogous writing products in prose (e.g., expository video or podcast segments that quote reliable sources, film scripts that have strong dialogue and dramatic tension)?	
a monologue, multimedia event, or script for any other live-performance medium	• allow room for the performer or host to contribute creatively, such as by interpreting the text in his or her own style?	
	• include delivery directions for performers where appropriate to signal emotion or volume?	
	• match the spoken text and content to the venue as well as to any other media elements (e.g. screen projections, music)?	
	• write material of the correct length so that speakers don't have to read your script too fast or too slowly?	
an oral history, reality TV–inspired video, or other documentary-style script	• respect the privacy of your subject(s) and honor any agreements, explicit or implicit, that you made previously?	
	• include strong voice-over or on-screen text transitions between video segments where necessary?	
	• appropriate media products from other sources in a way that complies with Fair Use guidelines or copyright regulations?	
a picture book or multimedia presentation with text	• consciously decide when you want the images and text to reinforce the same information and when you want them to diverge somewhat, with each element conveying complementary information?	
	• follow the basic strategies of visual storytelling that you know from fine art, comics, or film, and adapt them as needed?	
	• capitalize on any audio elements despite the central role of images and text? In multimedia this might mean an underlying music bed, and in a picture book it means the sound and texture of certain words as they are read aloud.	

Chapter 2: Audio Revision Checklist

Name: _____

Date: _____

If you are writing . . .	Did you make sure to . . .	✓
a multisegment podcast	• include a variety of types of segments to hold listener interest?	
	• script transitions between the segments?	
	• grab listeners' attention and tell them about what's coming up?	
	• make each segment stand on its own, using the writing strategies best suited to it (e.g., interview, radio drama, news spot, etc.)?	
	• welcome listeners with an intro and thank them in a wrap-up?	
a radio drama	• use sound effects and music to establish mood?	
	• include directions that help actors vary intensity, volume, and other elements of spoken word performances?	
	• choose words for maximum descriptive or dramatic impact—but ones that are also not too awkward to say or hard to understand?	
	• signal sudden shifts in time or place so that listeners can follow any leaps the story takes?	
	• use precise words in your delivery directions?	
a news broadcast or PSA	• edit your writing so information can be conveyed clearly and quickly?	
	• employ the strategies of effective expository writing (for news) and persuasive writing (for PSAs)?	
	• keep the tone of your script serious but conversational and avoid using fancy language inappropriately?	
	• write material of the correct length so that speakers don't have to read your script too fast or too slowly?	
a recorded poetry reading	• script an intro that identifies the title and author?	
	• feature music and sound effects that fit the poem's imagery, themes, and tone?	
	• include pauses and/or moments of silence that highlight the rhythms of the poem?	
	• divide the lines of poetry between readers, and provide delivery directions for each, in a way that underscores the poem's meaning (in scripts for multiple voices)?	

Chapter 3: Comics and Graphic Novel Revision Checklist

Name: _____

Date: _____

If you are writing . . .	Did you make sure to . . .	✓
a comic book or part of a graphic novel	• make the story flow from panel to panel?	
	• use a book map to plan each page with an eye to the additional content the reader will see on the same spread?	
	• support your dramatic structure by using medium-specific devices such as splash pages and page-flips?	
	• include sound effects to give your story an "audio" element?	
	• develop characters using a variety of strategies?	
	• decide which information is best conveyed by captions, word balloons, or thought bubbles?	
a full script	• write clear, detailed instructions for the artist, since he or she will be working mostly from the text you provide?	
	• use thumbnails or larger breakdowns as needed to indicate the kind and amount of dialogue or other text for a scene, page, or panel so the artist can leave enough room for word balloons and similar elements?	
	• provide precise directions to the artist or letterer about the kind of sound effects, fonts, and word balloon shapes to include so that these elements help convey the story's themes and drama?	
	• supply separate visual references for the artist, either character designs or, in nonfiction, photos or other visuals from your research?	
	• specify which details the artist is free to make up so you won't be surprised when you see the art?	
a rough script (in which dialogue is added after the art is rendered)	• block out the main action in a page-by-page manner so the artist knows roughly what needs to happen and when?	

Chapter 4: Movie and Television Revision Checklist

Name: _____

Date: _____

If you are writing . . .	Did you make sure to . . .	✓
a screenplay or teleplay	• remember to "show, don't tell," especially when it comes to characters' feelings?	
	• use visualization techniques to help you imagine what the audience will see, and create storyboards as needed to help you plan the order of your visuals?	
	• draft a script that shows an awareness of the needs of different jobs on a film or TV crew?	
	• use precise words and carefully chosen details to create memorable settings and appeal to the senses?	
	• follow the same basic principles of good fiction, such as story structure, as you would when writing a stage play or short story?	
	• tell the story visually whenever possible?	
a screenplay	• script a scene that stands on its own?	
	• obey the "1-minute rule" so readers know how long each scene, and the entire work, will run on the screen?	
	• show through action, setting, and other story elements instead of telling through dialogue?	
	• avoid "overdirecting" the film by including too many precise descriptions of shots, camera movements, and technical details?	
a teleplay	• obey the "1-minute rule" for dramatic episodes and a guideline of 30–40 seconds per page of a sitcom script or other shorter work?	
	• situate the episode in the context of a larger series—either an original series for which you have developed a "bible" or an existing series with which you have been careful to preserve continuity?	
	• structure your script to include breaks for commercials—and to introduce action before breaks to make viewers return afterward?	

Chapter 5: Digital Storytelling and Video Revision Checklist

Name: _____

Date: _____

If you are writing . . .	Did you make sure to . . .	✓
a PSA or commercial	• identify a target audience and write with it in mind?	
	• grab the viewer's attention?	
	• employ the strategies of effective persuasive writing (offering examples or supporting evidence and so on)?	
	• focus on key ideas by having both video and audio highlight them?	
	• avoid false or clearly exaggerated claims?	
	• include a call to action and tagline (for a PSA)?	
	• limit the content of your script so it fits in the allotted time when it's produced?	
a news spot	• answer the questions *Who? What? Where? When? Why? How?* for your audience?	
	• employ the strategies of effective expository writing (for example, clarity, concision, providing sources for facts, and so on)?	
	• pay attention to the tone, making sure that it is not too informal?	
	• use visuals, not just spoken words, to convey or expand upon some of the key information?	
	• avoid showing bias?	
a book trailer	• grab your audience's attention with a striking image, idea, or moment?	
	• summarize the main story elements while keeping the viewer hungry to learn more?	
	• preview the actual content of the book through quotes and images that illustrate it?	
	• use words and phrases with persuasive power much as movie trailers or other forms of commercials do?	
	• keep your tone enthusiastic and informal?	
a video poetry or digital scene adaptation	• identify the title and author?	
	• divide the original literary text into discrete chunks that appear as different sections within the two-column format?	
	• feature media elements that complement the text's imagery, themes, and tone?	
	• use graphics or text-on-screen when appropriate?	
	• focus on key words, phrases, and ideas and decide whether they are best presented as video, audio, or both?	

WRITING RUBRICS

A central tenet of this book is that scriptwriting can dovetail with, and even replace, many more traditional curricular assignments. Of course this could prompt questions related to assessment, since scripts may seem to represent strikingly new forms for which previous expectations and learning benchmarks might not apply. That's where the rubrics on the following pages come in. As you'll see, any given type of script aligns closely with the applicable standards for the related writing mode. Additionally, each script must function per its primary audience—as a text of practical writing. Both of these aspects of successful scripts are captured in the rubrics, although of course you are free to supplement them with more granular evaluative parameters drawn from the rubrics you may already be using. This speaks to the flexibility of scriptwriting in the classroom generally.

Moreover, you can reproduce and share these rubrics with students at any number of points in their scriptwriting journey: the realization that these assessment tools comprise so many of the conventional writing skills that students have already been working hard to master should be a comfort both to them and to you.

Scripts—General Application

4	3	2	1
Composition and Craft			
• Writing is clear and well organized. • Compelling themes (in fiction) or interesting main ideas (in nonfiction) are well supported throughout. • Voice, tone, and storytelling are engaging to the script's secondary audience. • Conventions for grammar, usage, and mechanics are consistently followed where permitted by the script format).	• Writing is usually clear and generally well organized. • Themes (in fiction) or main ideas (in nonfiction) are supported throughout. • Voice, tone, and storytelling are effective and sometimes engaging to the script's secondary audience. • Conventions for grammar, usage, and mechanics are mostly followed (exceptions allowed where permitted by the script format).	• Writing is insufficiently clear or organized to the point where viewers will sometimes be unable to follow ideas and information. • Themes (in fiction) or main ideas (in nonfiction) are evident but not always supported by incidents or examples. • Voice, tone, and storytelling are serviceable in terms of conveying information to the script's secondary audience. • Conventions for grammar, usage, and mechanics are sometimes followed.	• Writing lacks clarity or organization, making it largely impossible for viewers to follow ideas and information. • Themes (in fiction) or main ideas (in nonfiction) are not evident or not supported. • Voice, tone, and/or storytelling are absent or confusing to the script's secondary audience. • Conventions for grammar, usage, and mechanics are ignored or followed incorrectly.
Practical Value			
• Follows a recognizable script format or a combination of recognizable formats almost flawlessly. • Meets the needs of its primary audience by providing necessary information for collaborators or performers. • If applicable, the intended origin (e.g., researched/sampled, shot, drawn, spoken) of any specific piece of media is consistently clear to primary audience readers.	• Follows a recognizable format or a combination of recognizable formats; is easy for the primary audience to grasp. • Demonstrates an awareness of the needs of its primary audience by usually providing necessary information for collaborators or performers. • If applicable, the intended origin (e.g., researched/sampled, shot, drawn, spoken) of any specific piece of media is usually clear to primary audience readers.	• Follows some of the formatting conventions of a script but not always in a way that corresponds to a recognizable medium. • Does not meet some of the needs of its primary audience by providing necessary information for collaborators or performers. • If applicable, the intended origin (e.g., researched/sampled, shot, drawn, spoken) of any specific piece of media is sometimes clear to primary audience readers.	• Does not follow a recognizable script format or combination of formats. • Does not consistently meet the needs of its primary audience by providing necessary information for collaborators or performers. • If applicable, the intended origin (e.g., researched/sampled, shot, drawn, spoken) of any specific piece of media is rarely clear to primary audience readers.

Scripts—General Application

4	3	2	1
		Writing for the Medium	
• Consistently and effectively conveys information or tells a story through the sensory channels and experiential norms of the medium. • Employs the unique conventions and formal elements of the medium to their full advantage. • Demonstrates an awareness of its secondary audience's expectations for the medium and consistently exceeds them.	• Usually conveys information or tells a story through the sensory channels and experiential norms of the medium, sometimes effectively. • Generally employs the unique conventions and formal elements of the medium effectively. • Demonstrates an awareness of its secondary audience's expectations for the medium and consistently meets them.	• Disproportionately relies on certain sensory channels and experiential norms for the given medium. Examples might include an audio-visual medium in which sound is neglected or a performance-based medium that is heavy on dialogue but lacks compelling stage directions or visual interest. • Employs some of the unique conventions and formal elements of the medium but in a limited way that is sometimes incorrect. • Demonstrates some awareness of its secondary audience's expectations for the medium and sometimes meets them.	• Does not demonstrate an awareness of the sensory channels and experiential norms of the medium. Examples might include a script for a short film that consists entirely of on-screen text rather than moving images or a radio drama made up solely of the audio track of a video recording of a live performance. • Does not employ the unique conventions and formal elements of the medium, or does so incorrectly. • Demonstrates little or no awareness of its secondary audience's expectations for the medium and rarely, if ever, meets them.

Spoken Word and Audio Scripts

4	3	2	1
Composition and Craft			
• Writing is clear and well organized. • Compelling themes (in fiction) or interesting main ideas (in nonfiction) are well supported. • Voice, tone, and storytelling are engaging to listeners (the script's secondary audience). • Conventions for grammar, usage, and mechanics are consistently followed (exceptions allowed where permitted by the script format).	• Writing is usually clear and generally well organized. • Themes (in fiction) or main ideas (in nonfiction) are supported. • Voice, tone, and storytelling are effective and sometimes engaging to listeners (the script's secondary audience). • Conventions for grammar, usage, and mechanics are mostly followed (exceptions allowed where permitted by the script format).	• Writing is insufficiently clear or organized to the point where listeners won't always be able to follow ideas and information. • Themes (in fiction) or main ideas (in nonfiction) are evident but not always supported by incident or examples. • Voice, tone, and storytelling are serviceable in terms of conveying information to listeners (the script's secondary audience). • Conventions for grammar, usage, and mechanics are sometimes followed.	• Writing lacks clarity and/or organization, making it largely impossible for listeners to follow ideas and information. • Themes (in fiction) or main ideas (in nonfiction) are not evident or not supported. • Voice, tone, and/or storytelling are either absent or confusing to listeners (the script's secondary audience). • Conventions for grammar, usage, and mechanics are ignored or followed incorrectly.
Practical Value			
• Follows recognizable format for audio scripts almost flawlessly. • Meets the needs of its primary audience by providing necessary information for collaborators (actors, announcers, news readers, producers, technicians, and so on). • Specifies and describes audio elements in a way that is consistently feasible, effective, and clear, given the context and purpose of the script.	• Follows recognizable format for audio scripts; is easy for the primary audience to grasp. • Demonstrates an awareness of the needs of its primary audience by usually providing necessary information for collaborators (actors, announcers, news readers, producers, technicians, and so on). • Specifies and describes audio elements in a way that is usually feasible, effective, and clear, given the context and purpose of the script.	• Follows some of the formatting conventions for audio scripts. • Does not meet some of the needs of its primary audience by omitting some necessary information for collaborators (actors, announcers, news readers, producers, technicians, and so on). • Does not specify and describe audio elements often enough in a way that is feasible, effective, or clear, given the context and purpose of the script.	• Does not follow a recognizable format for audio scripts. • Does not consistently meet the needs of its primary audience by providing necessary information for collaborators (actors, announcers, news readers, producers, technicians, and so on). • Does not specify and describe audio elements appropriately, or does so in a way that is not feasible, effective, or clear, given the context and purpose of the script.

Spoken Word and Audio Scripts

4	3	2	1
Writing for the Medium			
• Speakers and segments are identified for listeners (the script's secondary audience), and thoughtful transitions consistently help them follow the flow of information. • Audio devices such as sound effects, music, and precisely chosen spoken words are used effectively throughout, often evoking the other senses. • Employs the formal elements of the medium to their full advantage; these include volume, tempo, emphasis, tone of voice, and so on.	• Speakers and/or segments are identified for listeners (the script's secondary audience), and transitions often help them follow the flow of information. • For the most part, audio devices such as sound effects, music, and precisely chosen spoken words are used effectively, sometimes evoking the other senses. • Occasionally employs the formal elements of the medium to their full advantage; these include volume, tempo, emphasis, tone of voice, and so on.	• Speakers and/or segments are rarely identified for listeners (the script's secondary audience), and transitions are often lacking that would help them follow the flow of information. • Audio devices such as sound effects, music, and precisely chosen spoken words are seldom used effectively, rarely evoking the other senses. • Rarely employs the formal elements of the medium to their full advantage; these include volume, tempo, emphasis, tone of voice, and so on.	• Speakers and/or segments are not identified or necessary transitions are lacking for listeners (the script's secondary audience), or does so in a way that is incorrect or confusing. • Audio devices such as sound effects, music, and precisely chosen spoken words are not evident, or are used ineffectively or inappropriately. • Does not employ the formal elements of the medium or does so inappropriately; these include volume, tempo, emphasis, tone of voice, and so on.

Comics and Graphic Novel Scripts

4	3	2	1
Composition and Craft			
• Writing is clear and well organized. • Compelling themes (in fiction) or interesting main ideas (in nonfiction) are well supported throughout. • Voice, tone, and storytelling are engaging for readers (the script's secondary audience). • Conventions for grammar, usage, and mechanics are consistently followed (exceptions allowed where permitted by the script format).	• Writing is usually clear and generally well organized. • Themes (in fiction) or main ideas (in nonfiction) are supported throughout. • Voice, tone, and storytelling are effective and sometimes engaging for readers (the script's secondary audience). • Conventions for grammar, usage, and mechanics are mostly followed (exceptions allowed where permitted by the script format).	• Writing is insufficiently clear or organized to the point where readers (secondary audience) will sometimes be unable to follow ideas and information. • Themes (in fiction) or main ideas (in nonfiction) are evident, but not always supported by incident or examples. • Voice, tone, and storytelling are serviceable in terms of conveying information to readers (the script's secondary audience). • Conventions for grammar, usage, and mechanics are sometimes followed.	• Writing lacks clarity and/or organization, making it largely impossible for (secondary audience) readers to follow ideas and information. • Themes (in fiction) and main ideas (in nonfiction) are either not evident or not supported. • Voice, tone, and/or storytelling are absent or confusing to readers (the script's secondary audience). • Conventions for grammar, usage, and mechanics are ignored or followed incorrectly.
Practical Value			
• Follows a recognizable format for comics scripts almost flawlessly. • Meets the needs of its primary audience by providing necessary information for collaborators (letterers, story editors, colorists, pencilers, and so on). • Supplies the right amount of visual detail for the artist—neither too prescriptive nor too vague.	• Follows a recognizable format for comics scripts; is easy for the primary audience to grasp. • Demonstrates an awareness of the needs of its primary audience by usually providing necessary information for collaborators (letterers, story editors, colorists, pencilers, and so on). • Mostly supplies the right amount of visual detail for the artist—only occasionally too prescriptive or too vague.	• Follows some of the formatting conventions for comics scripts. • Does not meet some of the needs of its primary audience by providing necessary information for collaborators (letterers, story editors, colorists, pencilers, and so on). • Sometimes supplies the right amount of visual detail for the artist but is often either too prescriptive or too vague.	• Does not follow a recognizable format for comics scripts. • Does not consistently meet the needs of its primary audience by providing necessary information for collaborators (letterers, story editors, colorists, pencilers, and so on). • Supplies either too much or too little detail for the artist, which diminishes the capacity of the collaborator to contribute creatively.

Comics and Graphic Novel Scripts

4	3	2	1
		Writing for the Medium	
• Word balloons, thought bubbles, narrative captions, and other text fields are used effectively. • The story is told visually as well as through text; the artwork is not simply illustrative. • Employs the unique conventions and formal elements of the medium to their full advantage; these include panels, sound effects, page-flips, splash pages, and so on.	• Word balloons, thought bubbles, narrative captions, and other text fields are used correctly, usually effectively. • For the most part, the story is told visually as well as through text; the artwork underscores or expands on the meaning of the print text. • Employs the unique conventions and formal elements of the medium correctly; these include panels, sound effects, page-flips, splash pages, and so on.	• Word balloons, thought bubbles, narrative captions, and other text fields are used appropriately. • The story features a combination of print and text, but each mode often seems to work independently, neither complementing nor supplementing the other. • Employs some of the unique conventions and formal elements of the medium but in a limited way that is sometimes incorrect; these include panels, sound effects, page-flips, splash pages, and so on.	• Word balloons, thought bubbles, narrative captions, and other text fields are used inappropriately or not at all. • The story is told with an overreliance on either the visual or the textual; it resembles a film storyboard or a picture book more than a comic. • Does not employ the unique conventions and formal elements of the medium; these include panels, sound effects, page-flips, splash pages, and so on.

Movie and Television Scripts

4	3	2	1
Composition and Craft			
• Writing is clear and well organized. • Compelling themes are well supported throughout. • Voice, tone, and storytelling are engaging for viewers (the script's secondary audience). • Conventions for grammar, usage, and mechanics are consistently followed (exceptions allowed where permitted by the script format).	• Writing is usually clear and generally well organized. • Themes are supported throughout. • Voice, tone, and storytelling are effective and sometimes engaging to viewers (the script's secondary audience). • Conventions for grammar, usage, and mechanics are mostly followed (exceptions allowed where permitted by the script format).	• Writing is insufficiently clear or organized to the point where viewers will sometimes be unable to follow ideas and information. • Themes are evident but not always supported by dramatic incident. • Voice, tone, and storytelling are serviceable in terms of conveying story elements to viewers (the script's secondary audience) but are rarely engaging. • Conventions for grammar, usage, and mechanics are sometimes followed.	• Writing lacks clarity and/or organization, making it largely impossible for viewers to follow ideas and information. • Themes are not evident or not supported by dramatic incident. • Voice, tone, and/or storytelling are absent, confusing, or do not engage viewers (the script's secondary audience). • Conventions for grammar, usage, and mechanics are ignored or followed incorrectly.
Practical Value			
• Follows a recognizable format for movie or television scripts almost flawlessly. • Meets the needs of its primary audience by providing necessary information for collaborators (actors, directors, producers, editors, camera operators, and designers). • Supplies the right amount of visual detail for the production crew—neither too prescriptive nor too vague.	• Follows a recognizable format for movie or television scripts; is easy for the primary audience to grasp. • Demonstrates an awareness of the needs of its primary audience by usually providing necessary information for collaborators (actors, directors, producers, editors, camera operators, and designers). • Usually supplies the right amount of visual detail for the production crew—neither too prescriptive nor too vague.	• Follows some of the formatting conventions for movie or television scripts. • Does not meet some of the needs of its primary audience by providing necessary information for collaborators (actors, directors, producers, editors, camera operators, and designers). • Sometimes supplies the right amount of visual detail for the production crew but is often too prescriptive or too vague.	• Does not follow a recognizable format for movie or television scripts. • Does not consistently meet the needs of its primary audience by providing necessary information for collaborators (actors, directors, producers, editors, camera operators, and designers). • Supplies either too much or too little detail for the production crew, which diminishes the capacity of collaborators to contribute creatively.

Movie and Television Scripts

4	3	2	1
	Writing for the Medium		
• Uses the format and concisely written text to make the script length conform to the planned running time of the finished film or TV episode. • Consistently tells the story visually as well as through dialogue. Actions and details of the setting effectively convey ideas and emotions. • Employs the unique conventions and formal elements of the medium to their full advantage; these include directions for delivery and action, descriptions of specific shots (when appropriate), scene "slugs" to show transitions in time and place, and so on.	• Uses the format and concisely written text to make the script length conform roughly to the planned running time of the finished film or TV episode. • Usually tells the story visually as well as through dialogue. Actions and details of the setting sometimes convey ideas and emotions. • Usually employs the unique conventions and formal elements of the medium effectively; these include directions for delivery and action, descriptions of specific shots (when appropriate), scene "slugs" to show transitions in time and place, and so on.	• Demonstrates an inefficient use of the format or a lack of concision so the script length inconsistently conforms to the planned running time of the finished film or TV episode. • Relies too much on dialogue to tell the story. Actions or details of setting rarely convey ideas and emotions. • Employs some of the unique conventions and formal elements of the medium but in a limited way that is sometimes incorrect; these include directions for delivery and action, descriptions of specific shots (where appropriate), scene "slugs" to show transitions in time and place, and so on.	• Demonstrates an inefficient use of the format and a lack of concision so the script length does not conform to the planned running time of the finished film or TV episode. • Mostly "tells" the story through dialogue rather than showing it visually. Neither actions nor details of setting are used to convey ideas and emotions. The script may resemble an audio script more than moving image media script. • Does not employ the unique conventions and formal elements of the medium, or does so incorrectly; these include directions for delivery and action, descriptions of specific shots (when appropriate), scene "slugs" to show transitions in time and place, and so on.

Digital Storytelling and Video Scripts

4	3	2	1
Composition and Craft			
• Writing is clear and well organized. • Compelling themes (in fiction) or interesting main ideas (in nonfiction) are well supported throughout. • Voice, tone, and storytelling are engaging to the script's secondary audience. • Conventions for grammar, usage, and mechanics are consistently followed (exceptions allowed where permitted by the script format).	• Writing is usually clear and generally well organized. • Themes (in fiction) or main ideas (in nonfiction) are supported throughout. • Voice, tone, and storytelling are effective and sometimes engaging to the script's secondary audience. • Conventions for grammar, usage, and mechanics are mostly followed (exceptions allowed where permitted by the script format).	• Writing is insufficiently clear or organized to the point where viewers will sometimes be unable to follow ideas and information. • Themes (in fiction) or main ideas (in nonfiction) are evident, but not always supported by incidents or examples. • Voice, tone, and storytelling are serviceable in terms of conveying information to the script's secondary audience. • Conventions for grammar, usage, and mechanics are sometimes followed.	• Writing lacks clarity or organization, making it largely impossible for viewers to follow ideas and information. • Themes (in fiction) or main ideas (in nonfiction) are not evident or not supported. • Voice, tone, and/or storytelling are absent or confusing to the script's secondary audience. • Conventions for grammar, usage, and mechanics are ignored or followed incorrectly.
Practical Value			
• Follows a recognizable format for video or digital storytelling scripts almost flawlessly. • Meets the needs of its primary audience by providing necessary information for collaborators (researchers, voice-over readers, editors, designers/artists, technicians, and so on). • The intended origin (e.g., researched/sampled, shot, drawn, spoken) of any specific piece of media is consistently clear to primary audience readers.	• Follows a recognizable format for video or digital storytelling scripts; is easy for the primary audience to grasp. • Demonstrates an awareness of the needs of its primary audience by usually providing necessary information for collaborators (researchers, voice-over readers, on-camera speakers, editors, designers/artists, technicians, and so on). • The intended origin (e.g., researched/sampled, shot, drawn, spoken) of any specific piece of media is usually clear to primary audience readers.	• Follows some of the formatting conventions for video or digital storytelling scripts. • Does not meet some of the needs of its primary audience by providing necessary information for collaborators (researchers, voice-over readers, on-camera speakers, editors, designers/artists, technicians, and so on). • The intended origin (e.g., researched/sampled, shot, drawn, spoken) of any specific piece of media is sometimes clear to primary audience readers.	• Does not follow a recognizable format for video or digital storytelling scripts. • Does not consistently meet the needs of its primary audience by providing necessary information for collaborators (researchers, voice-over readers, on-camera speakers, editors, designers/artists, technicians, and so on). • The intended origin (e.g., researched/sampled, shot, drawn, spoken) of any specific piece of media is rarely clear to primary audience readers.

Digital Storytelling and Video Scripts

4	3	2	1
Writing for the Medium			
• Images and sound are used effectively throughout; subcategories (graphics, moving-image video, music, voice-over, sound effects, text-on-screen, and so on) are appropriate, consistently engaging, and/or informative.	• Images and sound are used throughout; subcategories (graphics, moving-image video, music, voice-over, sound effects, text-on-screen, and so on) are usually appropriate, engaging, and/or informative.	• Images and sound are used but not always effectively; subcategories (graphics, moving-image video, music, voice-over, sound effects, text-on-screen, and so on) are rarely appropriate, engaging, and/or informative.	• Images or sound, or both, are not used effectively throughout; subcategories (graphics, moving-image video, music, voice-over, sound effects, text-on-screen, and so on) are not used appropriately or do not convey information or ideas clearly.
• The script consistently matches audio and visual elements so that each supports or complements the other.	• For the most part, the script consistently matches audio and visual elements so that each supports or complements the other.	• The script features a combination of audio and visual elements, but often these do not clearly support or complement each other.	• The script relies too much on audio or visual elements; attempts to make audio and visual elements complement the other are confusing or ineffective.
• Employs the conventions and formal elements of the medium (paper editing of visuals and audio, informative/impactful text spoken or displayed on screen) to grab the secondary audience's attention and communicate effectively.	• Employs the conventions and formal elements of the medium (paper editing of visuals and audio, informative/impactful text spoken or displayed on screen), sometimes grabbing the secondary audience's attention and generally communicating effectively.	• Employs the conventions and formal elements of the medium (paper editing of visuals and audio, informative/impactful text spoken or displayed on screen) inconsistently, rarely grabbing the secondary audience's attention or communicating effectively.	• Does not employ the conventions and formal elements of the medium (paper editing of visuals and audio, informative/impactful text spoken or displayed on screen) to grab the secondary audience's attention or communicate effectively.

Glossary of Scriptwriting and Media Terms

A-roll: Footage consisting of interviews, documented events, and images tied to specific script content that is of primary importance to the narrative.

act: A substantial dramatic section of a stage play, screenplay, or teleplay.

ambient sound: Background sound recorded live; a type of SOT (*see entry for* SOT) that can help establish a setting, set a mood, or allow greater clarity for voice-over, music, or sound effects.

anchor: The main news reader and host for an audio or video news program.

animation: The illusion of movement created when any image is presented as moving when, in fact, no real-time movement is being recorded/captured (not simply what might be thought of as a "cartoon").

audio: Media content that is created for audiences to listen to only, such as radio broadcasts or MP3 files; alternately, the aural component of a media product (e.g., the audio track of a video).

B-roll: Footage that can be used as filler; often visible over A-roll audio (i.e., key quotes taken from an interview conducted expressly for a video) as a way of illustrating a speaker's points or topic instead of simply showing the speaker on camera.

beat: A parenthetical delivery direction used to signal a very brief pause in plays, teleplays, and screenplays, such as when the audience is to notice that something suddenly occurs to a character.

beauty shot: Stunning but nonessential image that adds visual appeal to a video.

bias: A personal or editorial viewpoint that affects the reporting of facts or the presentation of information; a reflection (present in all media messages, to some degree) of the conscious choices of the makers regarding what to include or to omit.

bird's-eye view: Extreme overhead point of view providing a literal "overview" of the action or setting in a way that shows where things are in relation to each other.

blocking: Process of planning where actors will stand and move in relation to each other and objects downstage (the side of a theater's stage that is nearest the audience).

break: Announcement or stand-alone musical piece that serves as a break between segments; also known as *interlude*.

breakdowns/thumbnails: Rough sketches, often created by an artist and writer together, that show how the action and plot points in a comics story will "break down" on a page-by-page and panel-by-panel basis; diminutive breakdowns are sometimes called "thumbnails."

camera angle: The position of a camera in relation to the subject being shot, thus affecting the audience's view of it.

caption/caption box: Print text that accompanies, supports, or translates a visual. In comics, the rectangular boxes that appear along the top or bottom edges of a panel; the text inside can represent the author's voice providing narration, simple transitions, or more involved information, especially in graphic nonfiction.

close-up: Shot in which the camera is near the subject.

comics: The medium of sequential art narratives, both fiction or nonfiction; the term comprises closely related subcategories, such as comic books, comic strips, graphic novels, and manga.

contact info: A means by which the producers of a piece of media can be reached by their audience; an e-mail address should be sufficient.

cue: Signal for a type of audio in a script.

cut: Transition between shots in any medium with moving images.

cut scene: A brief scene that automatically plays during a video game, usually as a bridge between setting or levels of gameplay.

dead air: Extended period in a broadcast or transmission without any sound and/or video whatsoever.

digital storytelling: A computer-based "movie" usually consisting of digitized still photos accompanied by voice-over narration (often of a personal nature); a form of multimedia presentation.

director: Person in charge of a collaborative media project, whether for the stage, screen, or airwaves. Typically the director coordinates both the performative and technical aspects of a production in a direct, hands-on manner.

dissolve: When one shot in moving-image media replaces another by fading out while another fades in; dissolve effects can also be used with static images presented in digital stories.

double-page splash: In comics, two splash pages (*see entry for* splash page) facing each other in a single spread.

downstage: That side of a theater's stage that is nearest the audience.

establishing shot: A shot in visual narratives that quickly establishes the location of a subsequent, and usually indoor, scene.

fade in/fade out: A transitional device used in both audio and visual media. With audio, it denotes gradually increasing or decreasing the volume of a track; with film and video, it means increasing or decreasing the visibility of a shot.

Fair Use: Legal principle that grants exception to copyright protections when the benefits to society outweigh the interests of the rights holder; use of mass media in education, and student projects in particular, usually fall into this category.

fan fiction: Fiction created by fans as an unauthorized addition to an existing, professionally published or commercially broadcast work; common in prose form, fan fiction can also surface in the context of videos, comics, and other script formats.

flashback: In any narrative medium and genre, a leap backward in the story's chronology before resuming in its normal direction.

flash-forward: In any narrative medium and genre, a leap forward in the story's chronology. To spark audience interest, some scriptwriters begin with a flash-forward in the form of a prologue.

Foley art: A type of sound effect that is made with practical– not electronic or digital–means (e.g., a coconut shell clapped together for the sound of striking horse hoofs).

format: In scriptwriting, the particular layout of text on the page that reflects the needs of a specific medium and the conventions that have arisen to address them.

graphic: Any still image, art, or designed text used in a video, digital story, print advertisement, and so on; lettering in comics is also considered a graphic.

heading: Text used to indicate the beginning of a new scene or act, sometimes called a "scene heading"; these appear in all caps in scripts across media. For screenplays and teleplays they are formatted flush left and called "sluglines"; in stage play scripts they are centered on the page.

ID: Brief reminder to listeners of the show or station they're listening to. IDs are more common in radio because in television there are usually visual reminders either in the background or at the bottom of the screen.

insert: A shot in moving-image media that quickly draws attention to an item before returning to the main action; often used for text to be read by the audience, such as handwritten notes, newspapers, or wristwatches.

interlude: (*see entry for* break)

intertitle: A shot in film or video in which only text appears on screen, as in the dialogue for silent films.

intro: Short for "introduction"; lines spoken by a host or narrator to set up a given video or audio segment or to open a podcast.

line: Spoken text, not directions or cues, as in a stage play.

MP3: File format most popular for sharing digital music files.

media: Plural form of *medium.*

medium: A vehicle for meaning-making and communication.

medium shot: A camera shot (or the image equivalent in comics) between a close-up and a long or distance shot, usually capturing most, but not all, of a person's body.

moving shot: A shot that follows a character while he or she is walking, running, or otherwise actively moving; indicated as "MOVING" in most scripts.

moving-image media: Media that relies on the illusion of movement created by static images presented in rapid succession; examples include television, film, and most forms of video.

multimedia: In theory, any medium that includes elements from at least one other medium; in practice, a medium that presents products from other media in succession or juxtaposition, such as certain digital storytelling, live presentations, and websites.

music bed: Music over which speech or other audio is heard.

news spot: A brief piece of video or audio that delivers a single news story.

off: When appearing parenthetically next to a character's name, it signals that the following dialogue should be spoken "offstage"; for screen media the equivalent is *O.S.* (for "off-screen") and in comics the same effect is achieved via *O.P.* ("off-panel").

off-mike/off-mic: Delivery direction indicating that a line should sound distant, mumbled, or otherwise indistinct to the listener.

off-panel (O.P.): Refers to action or speakers not directly shown in a comics panel.

off-screen (O.S.): When someone is speaking off-screen but could conceivably enter the viewable space; similar to "off-panel" in comics and, less so, to "off-mic" in audio; differs from a voice-over.

on-air promo: An advertisement for a TV show that appears on television, or for an audio program that appears during another audio program.

outro: A wrap-up of an individual segment; opposite of an intro.

over-the-shoulder shot: Shot composed as if standing right behind someone, usually a speaker in a conversation or interview.

narrative box (*see entry for* caption/caption box)

page-flip: Key "breaking" device used in comics' story structure; a page-flip can introduce new settings and characters without using transitional text.

pan: Short for "panorama"; horizontal movement of the camera.

panel: Basic storytelling unit of comics.

paper edit: The idea of editing a video in script form (because the visual and sound elements are clearly described and organized) instead of editing it after the fact, after video has already been shot or compiled.

platform: The physical/technological means by which media products are disseminated (e.g., film is a medium, but movies can be delivered by broadcast, Internet streaming, DVD, or theatrical projection–all different platforms).

POV: Short for "point of view"; a shot that seems to be subjective, meaning that the camera is used as a surrogate for the vision of someone who appears on screen.

podcast: Downloadable audio or video files than can be played on computers or, commonly, on mobile playing devices such as Apple's iPod.

producer: The creative organizer of, and often the driving force behind, a media production; producers can be project managers but also collaborative partners who offer input on scripts to ensure that they match the intended target audience.

public service announcement (PSA): Brief informational/persuasive message that is provided for the perceived benefit of the listening/watching public.

pull quote: A compelling or eye-catching quote pulled from a main text, often an interview, and highlighted for the audience.

reaction shot: A composition in visual narratives in which the reaction of a person or character is shown.

scene: Dramatic action that occurs within a single place and time period; the structural units that make up an act.

screenplay: A script used for feature films and shorts; though the term is occasionally used for documentaries, it is a better fit for fictional works (note the word *play*, inherited from stage dramas).

script: Text used by performers, technicians, and producers to guide the creation of a media product; can be fiction or nonfiction.

segment: The breakdown of episodes (e.g., podcasts) into smaller sections, each with its own theme.

semi-splash: In a comic, a half-page splash used to underscore dramatic moments (*see entry for* splash page); often used at the end of a chapter or issue to heighten the impact of a cliffhanger.

shot: Single continuous running of the camera.

slugline: A scene heading in a teleplay or screenplay that briefly describes the setting; sometimes shortened to "slug."

SOT: Stands for "sound on tape" as distinct from sound that wasn't captured as part of the videotaping process, such as voice-over narration or added music.

sound bite: Brief audio excerpt of a longer recording; can be incorporated into what is otherwise a scripted piece, as in a news spot.

sound effects/SFX: Aural elements that are intentionally added to a media product beyond the sounds resulting naturally from a performance or ambient conditions; in comics, this includes the arrangement of oversized block letters to denote a sound effect (e.g., CRASH! for a crashing sound); in other media, also can be used for laughter ("Ha ha ha"), songs and music, and anything else writers want readers to "hear" apart from spoken dialogue.

spec: To provide specifications (a detailed description) for a piece of media to be created or to be located and supplied if it already exists.

speech balloon: (*see entry for* word balloon)

splash page: Page in a typical comic book that features a striking, dramatic image to pull readers into the story, usually the first page; used less often in graphic novels.

spread break: In print media, break between the bottom of a left-hand page and the top of the opposite right-hand page; comics writers often use this natural pause in reading to start a new scene or shift the setting without using a caption to alert readers.

stage left: Positional directions for a theatrical cast and crew. As with *stage right*, the perspective is that of the actors; stage left is thus to the audience's right.

stage right: Positional directions for a theatrical cast and crew. As with *stage left*, the perspective is that of the actors; stage right is thus to the audience's left.

tagline: A memorable catchphrase or slogan, usually for a media product, publisher, or advertised commodity.

teaser: A shortened form of advertising that "teases" the audience; often employed because the existing content or available time for the commercial is limited.

teleplay: A script used for dramatic and comedic television episodes; though scripts are used for television news programs and advertisements, they are not teleplays, which are fictional.

thought bubble: A text field conveying a character's private thoughts, usually with a trail of bubbles in diminishing size leading back to the character's head; iconic images such as dark clouds and Valentine's Day–style hearts can be inserted into a thought bubble to express emotions graphically.

trailer: Commercial advertisement for a forthcoming media product, usually a film or book, that is delivered via moving-image media or multimedia; so named because previews of coming attractions used to follow, or "trail," the feature movie presentation in theaters.

two-shot: An image, moving (video) or static (comics), in which two people/characters are depicted, often in conversation or other forms of interaction; an alternative to presenting alternating images of each person.

upstage: That side of a theater's stage that is farthest from the audience.

video: Technically, a medium that relies on the digital capture of images to create the impression of movement; in the information and entertainment industries, it is distinguished from film by being less expensive and easier to manipulate; in scriptwriting, a medium that relies on a two-column format, typically making use of preexisting film or video sources.

voice-over: Narration spoken "over" other content, usually still or moving images; voice-over can be delivered by a fictional character in a style similar to first-person narration in prose or by a journalist or authorial voice in nonfiction contexts; in film and television, voice-over is distinguished from an off-screen or off-camera speaker because in the latter the speaker is simply not shown in a shot but conceivably could still become visible.

webisode: An episode of a web-based "TV" show that can be accessed by streaming or through download; the term does not apply to regular TV series that are made available online subsequent to television broadcast.

wipe cut: Cut achieved by one image/shot wiping away and replacing the previous image; a common video effect.

word balloon: The balloon-shaped text field in a comic in which dialogue appears, with a "tail" pointing toward the speaker.

worm's-eye view: Image with a perspective taken at ground level; used for dramatic effect to make characters or settings seem "bigger than life."

zoom: Diminution of the distance between viewer and subject of a shot through the action of the lens, not by moving the camera closer; used in scripts (sparingly) for sudden emphasis.

REFERENCES

Applebee, A. N., & Langer, J. A. (1983). Instructional scaffolding: Reading and writing as natural language activities. *Language Arts, 60*(2), 168–175.

Baker, F. *The media literacy clearinghouse.* Retrieved from http://frankwbaker.com/

Boothe, D., & Caspary, A. (2011). Reader's Theatre. *READ Magazine, 2,* 40–41.

Center for Digital Storytelling. (2013). *Mission.* Retrieved from http://www.storycenter.org/mission-vision/

Condon, W., & Rutz, C. (2012, December). A taxonomy of writing across the curriculum programs: Evolving to serve broader agendas. *College Composition and Communication, 64*(2), 357–382.

Echevarria, J., Vogt, M. E., & Short, D. (2004). *Making content comprehensible for English language learners: The SIOP model* (2nd ed.). Boston, MA: Allyn & Bacon.

Fleischman, P. (1988). *Joyful noise: Poems for two voices.* New York, NY: HarperCollins.

Fountas, I., & Pinnell, G. S. (1996). *Guided reading: Good first teaching for all students.* Portsmouth, NH: Heinemann.

Gardner, H. (2011). *Frames of mind: The theory of multiple intelligences.* New York, NY: Basic Books.

Hanauer, D. I., & Rivers, D. (2004). *Poetry and the meaning of life: Reading and writing poetry in language arts classrooms* (Vol. 38). Don Mills, Canada: Pippin.

Hobbs, R. (2010). *Copyright clarity: How fair use supports digital learning.* Thousand Oaks, CA: Corwin.

Jacobs, D. (2007). More than words: Comics as a means of teaching multiple literacies. *English Journal, 96*(3), 19–25.

Jacobs, H. H. (2010, July). *A new essential curriculum for a new time.* Talk delivered at the Partnership for Global Learning Conference, Rockville, MD. Retrieved from http://www.slideshare.net/internationaled/new-essential-curriculum-for-a-new-time

Jaffe, M., & Monnin, K. (2012). *Using content-area graphic texts for learning.* N. Mankato, MN: Maupin House.

Kaiser Family Foundation. (2003). *Key facts: Media literacy.* Menlo Park, CA: Henry J. Kaiser Family Foundation (Publication No. 3383). Retrieved from http://www.kff.org/entmedia/upload/key-facts-media-literacy.pdf

Koch, H., & Froelick, A. (1938). *The war of the worlds.* Retrieved from http://www.radio-heardhere.com/waroftheworlds/wotw-script.html [Please note that this appears to be a transcription of the radio drama and not the original script.]

McCloud, S. (1993). *Understanding comics: The invisible art.* Northampton, MA: Tundra.

Miller, S. M. (2010). Towards a multimodal literacy pedagogy: Digital video composing as 21st century literacy. In P. Albers & J. Sanders (Eds.), *Literacies, art, and multimodality* (pp. 254–281). Urbana-Champaign, IL: National Council of Teachers of English.

National Council of Teachers of English (NCTE). (2005, September). Using comics and graphic novels in the classroom. *The Council Chronicle*. Retrieved from http://www.ncte.org/magazine/archives/122031

National Council of Teachers of English (NCTE). (2008). *Code of best practices in fair use for media literacy education*. Urbana, IL: National Association for Media Literacy Education (NAMLE), Student Television Network (STN), Media Commission of the National Council of Teachers of English (NCTE), Action Coalition for Media Education (ACME), and Visual Communication Division of the International Communication Association (ICA). Retrieved from http://www.ncte.org/positions/statements/fairusemedialiteracy

National Governors Association Center for Best Practices & Council of Chief State School Officers. (2010). *Common core state standards for English language arts and literacy in history/social studies, science, and technical subjects*. Washington, DC: Author. Retreived from www.corestandards.org/assets/CCSSI_ELA%20Standards.pdf

Rasinski, T. (1990). Effects of repeated reading and listening-while-reading on reading fluency. *Journal of Educational Research, 83*(3), 147–150.

Routman, R. (2000). *Conversations: Strategies for teaching, learning, and evaluating*. Portsmouth, NH: Heinemann.

Shamburg, C. (2010). *Student-powered podcasting: Teaching for 21st-century literacy*. Washington, DC: International Society for Technology in Education (ISTE).

Share, J. (2009). *Media literacy is elementary: Teaching youth to critically read and create media*. New York, NY: Peter Lang.

Slagle, P. (1997, Summer). Getting real: Authenticity in writing prompts. *The Quarterly, 19*(3), 20–23.

Stansbury, M. (2010, February). Learning-style research under fire. *eSchool News, 13*(2), 1, 36.

Taguchi, E., Takayasu-Maass, M., & Gorsuch, G. J. (2004). Developing reading fluency in EFL: How assisted repeated reading and extensive reading affect fluency development. *Reading in a Foreign Language, 16*(2), 70–96.

INDEX

ABOUT THE AUTHOR

Peter Gutiérrez is a former English and social studies teacher, as well as a former professional scriptwriter, who has spent the past decade aligning curricula with high-interest media. His writings on this topic have appeared in *School Library Journal*, the *ALAN Review*, *Language Arts*, *Screen Education*, and many other publications. His consulting clients include Pearson, Scholastic Education, and Sesame Workshop.

Printed and bound by CPI Group (UK) Ltd, Croydon, CR0 4YY

09/06/2025

14685981-0005